BODY OPPONENT BAG
COMBINATIONS

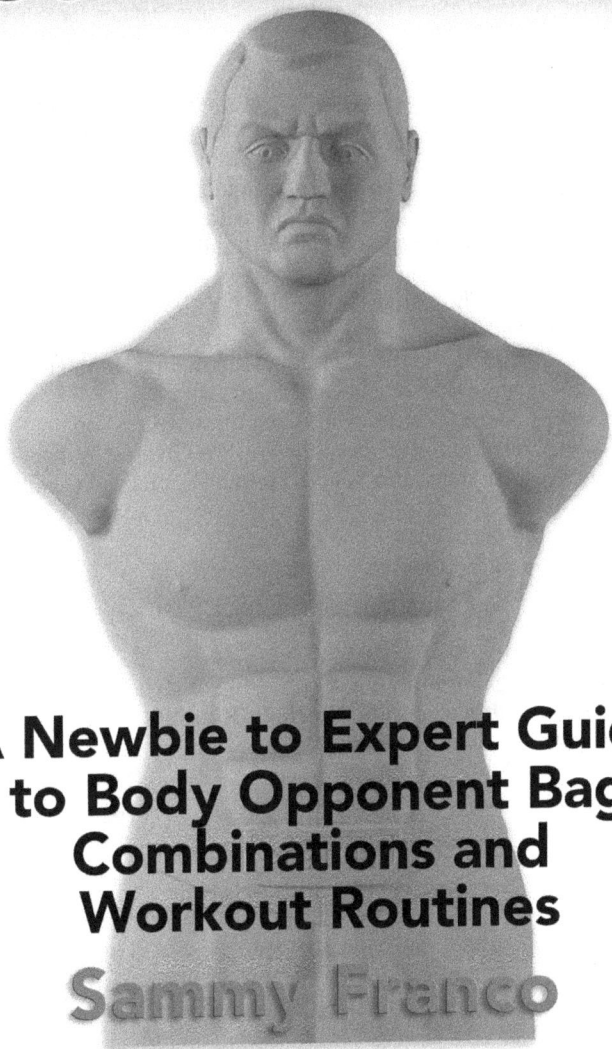

A Newbie to Expert Guide to Body Opponent Bag Combinations and Workout Routines

Sammy Franco

Also by Sammy Franco

The Complete Body Opponent Bag Book
Heavy Bag Workout
Heavy Bag Combinations
Heavy Bag Training
The Heavy Bag Bible
Invincible: Mental Toughness Techniques for Peak Performance
Knife Fighting: A Step-by-Step Guide to Practical Knife Fighting for Self-Defense
Cane Fighting
The Widow Maker Compendium
Unleash Hell: A Step-by-Step Guide to Devastating Widow Maker Combinations
Feral Fighting: Advanced Widow Maker Fighting Techniques
The Widow Maker Program: Extreme Self-Defense for Deadly Force Situations
Savage Street Fighting: Tactical Savagery as a Last Resort
Stand and Deliver: A Street Warrior's Guide to Tactical Combat Stances
Maximum Damage: Hidden Secrets Behind Brutal Fighting Combinations
First Strike: End a Fight in Ten Seconds or Less!
The Bigger They Are, The Harder They Fall
Self-Defense Tips and Tricks
Kubotan Power: Quick & Simple Steps to Mastering the Kubotan Keychain
Gun Safety: For Home Defense and Concealed Carry
Out of the Cage: A Guide to Beating a Mixed Martial Artist on the Street
Warrior Wisdom: Inspiring Ideas from the World's Greatest Warriors
War Machine: How to Transform Yourself Into a Vicious and Deadly Street Fighter
1001 Street Fighting Secrets
When Seconds Count: Self-Defense for the Real World
Killer Instinct: Unarmed Combat for Street Survival
Street Lethal: Unarmed Urban Combat

Body Opponent Bag Combinations: A Newbie to Expert Guide to Body Opponent Bag Combinations and Workout Routines
Copyright © 2018 by Sammy Franco
ISBN: 978-1-941845-66-0
Printed in the United States of America

Published by Contemporary Fighting Arts, LLC.
Visit us Online at: **ContemporaryFightingArts.com**

Contents

About This Book   VII

Chapter 1: The Body Opponent Bag   1

Chapter 2: BOB Set Up & Equipment   11

Chapter 3: Targets and Techniques   27

Chapter 4: Beginner Combinations   53

Chapter 5: Intermediate Combinations   75

Chapter 6: Advanced Combinations   99

Chapter 7: Body Opponent Bag Workouts   121

Body Opponent Bag Resources   150

Glossary   155

About Sammy Franco   185

"Take things as they are. Punch when you have to punch. Kick when you have to kick."

– Bruce Lee

Disclaimer

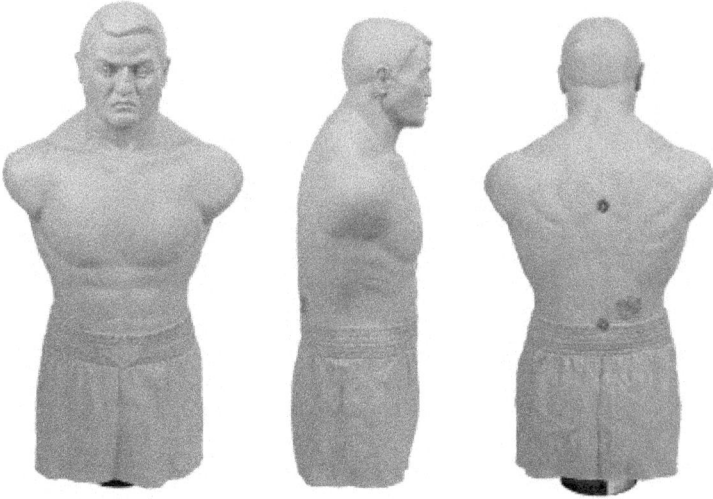

The information and techniques in this book can be dangerous and could lead to serious injury. The author, publisher, and distributors of this book disclaim any liability from loss, injury, or damage, personal or otherwise, resulting from the information and procedures in this book. This book is for academic study only.

Before you begin any exercise program, including those suggested in this book, it is important to check with your physician to see whether you have any condition that might be aggravated by strenuous exercise.

About This Book

Body Opponent Bag Combinations is the second book in my best-selling Body Opponent Bag Training Series. This one-of-a-kind book is a complete guide to mastering devastating punching combinations that will dramatically improve your fighting skills, condition your body, and breathe new life into your Body Opponent Bag workouts.

The workout routines featured in this book will also help you achieve maximum training performance in a variety of activities including, boxing, mixed martial arts, kick boxing, self-defense, and personal fitness.

This book also provides step-by-step instructions for performing beginner, intermediate and advanced BOB combination workouts. Many experienced fighters will find these punching combinations very challenging. However, the best feature of this book is that it teaches you how to create an unlimited number of Body Opponent Bag workout programs filled with an infinite amount of unique punching and kicking combinations.

The techniques featured in this book are based on my 30+ years of research, training and teaching the martial arts and combat sciences. I have taught these unique punching combinations to thousands of students, and I'm confident they will help you reach higher levels of training performance.

Body Opponent Bag Combinations has four chapters, each one

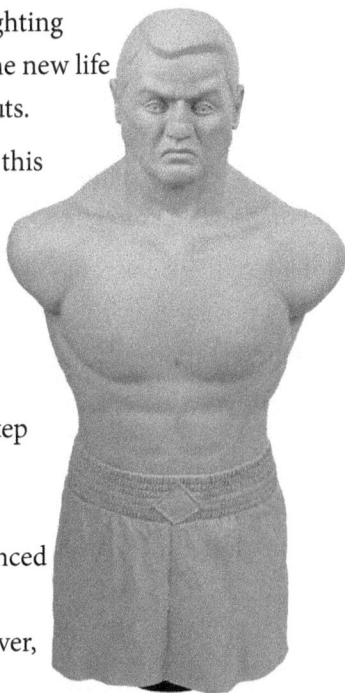

covers a critical aspect of training. This book assumes you currently possess the basic fighting skills. However, for those of you who need a quick refresher course, I have provided step-by-step instructions for all of the techniques in this book.

In addition, you will also find a glossary of terms. Since this is both a skill-building workbook and training guide, feel free to write in the margins, underline passages, and dog-ear the pages.

I encourage you to read this book from beginning to end, chapter by chapter. Only after you have read the entire book should you treat it as a reference and skip around, reading those chapters or combinations that directly apply to you.

Finally, this book is based on my best selling book, The Complete Body Opponent Bag. Therefore, if you want to know more about the many hidden training features of the body opponent bag, I suggest picking up a copy.

Train hard!

Sammy Franco
ContemporaryFightingArts.com

Chapter 1
The Body Opponent Bag

Body Opponent Bag Combinations

A One-Of-A-Kind Punching Bag

If you don't already know by now, the body opponent bag or BOB is a unique punching bag that's favored among self-defense practitioners, kick boxers, and martial artists of all styles and backgrounds. The BOB, however, is also becoming very popular with the general public who wants to relieve stress, improve their overall fitness, and pick up a few fighting skills along the way.

With so many different types of punching bags on the market, it becomes a bit confusing as to exactly what distinguishes the body opponent bag from other punching bags.

Some common question that often come up when considering using the Body Opponent Bag. What are the benefits of working out on the body opponent bag? What are the drawbacks? Exactly how do you use this lifelike punching bag? All of these questions, plus much more will be answered in this book.

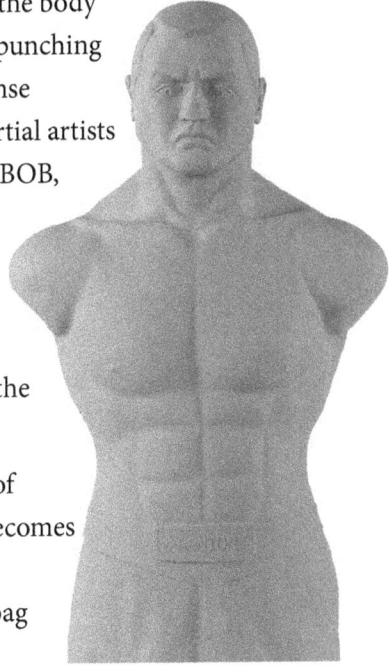

Exactly What is a Body Opponent Bag?

The body opponent bag is a self-standing lifelike punching bag designed to withstand tremendous punishment by allowing the practitioner to attack it with a wide variety of offensive techniques.

Essentially, the body opponent bag is made up of two parts: the torso and base. The torso is constructed of synthetic rubber material called plastisol and it can withstand tremendous abuse. In fact, my body opponent bag has been used daily for over fifteen years and it has never needed to be repaired or replaced.

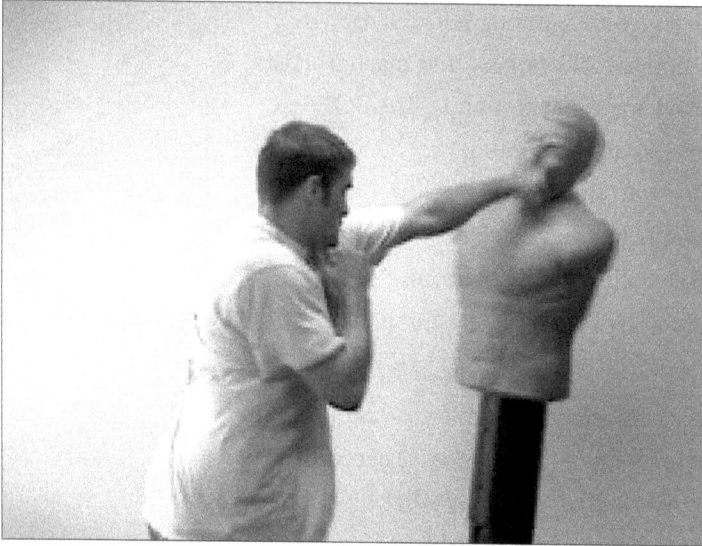

The Torso

The torso of the body opponent bag is life-size, measuring approximately forty inches in height and twenty-three inches in width. While its interior is filled with durable, thick foam material. While the torso is durable and resistant to punches and kicks, it still can be punctured with sharp objects, so be careful when handling it.

The Base

The base of the body opponent bag is constructed of hollow, hard plastic and it serves four purposes. First, it provides the necessary support to hold the mannequin in place. Second, it allows you to adjust the torso at various height levels. Third, when filled with either water or sand, it provides the torso with the necessary weight and resistance. Finally, the base allows you to move and transport the bob easily.

Unlike the traditional heavy bag, the BOB is self-standing and doesn't need to be hung from the ceiling or affixed to a stand. This is particularly appealing to people who have limited space when training. When the base is completely filled, it will weigh approximately 270 pounds.

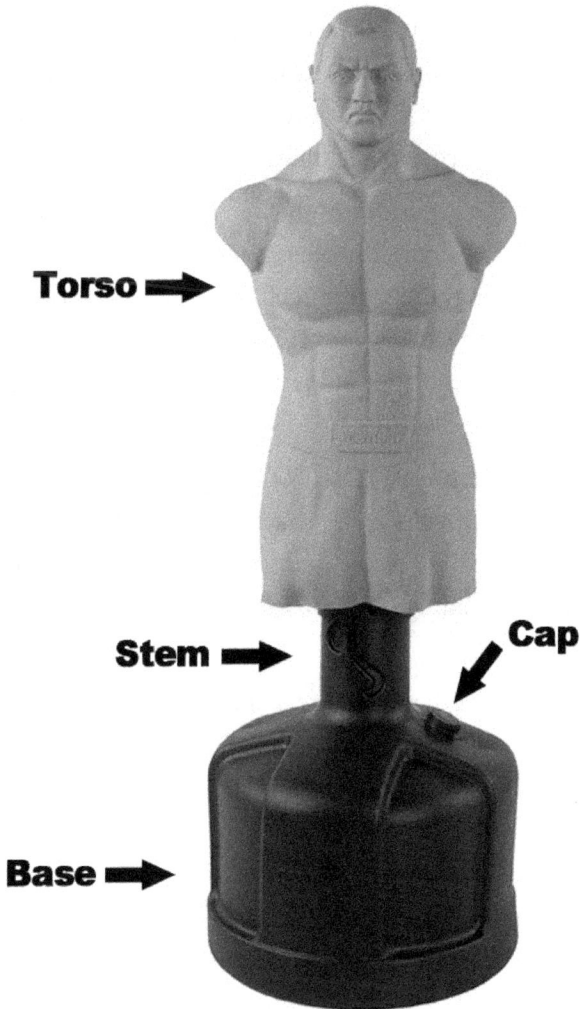

Torso ➡

Stem ➡   ↙ **Cap**

Base ➡

Benefits of BOB Training

The body opponent bag is a unique piece of training equipment that provides a wide range of benefits for the practitioner. In this section, I will discuss some of the many benefits that come from working out on the bag.

Developing Fighting Technique

The body opponent bag is a fantastic piece of equipment for developing your fighting skills and techniques. Compared to the traditional heavy bag, the BOB is a more specialized punching bag that develops a broader scope of techniques.

"Punching Bag" is a generic term that refers to a wide range of punching bags. For example, the double end bag is used for developing speed, timing, and fighting reflexes. This punching bag does have its purpose, but is doesn't hold a candle to the body opponent bag. In this photo, the author performs a horizontal elbow strike on the double end bag.

As you can imagine, a wide variety of kicks, punches, and strikes can be developed and ultimately perfected on the bag. However, the primary purpose of the BOB is to develop target accuracy for your striking techniques including jabs, crosses, hooks, uppercuts, elbow, and knee strikes.

There are, however, other fighting techniques that can be trained on the body opponent bag. Some include:

- Eye jabs
- Eye rakes
- Eye gouges
- Knife hand strikes
- Palm heels

- Bicep pops
- Head butts
- Hammer fists
- Tearing techniques
- Ground fighting skills
- Scenario based self-defense training
- Chokes and neck crank techniques

Developing Weapon Skills

Because of its lifelike features, the body opponent bag permits you to perform hand held weapons training. For example, you can practice stick strikes, knife attacks, kubotan techniques, and even pepper spray training on the bag. Just be certain to use the right equipment when training or you can permanently damage the bag.

Developing Fighting Attributes

Fighting attributes are unique qualities that enhance or amplify a particular fighting technique. They might include: speed, power, timing, agility, ambidexterity, coordination, combat conditioning as well as many others.

The body opponent bag is an ideal piece of equipment for developing some of these fighting attributes. They include some of the following:

- Proper Targeting
- Ambidexterity
- Offensive timing
- Balance and coordination
- Footwork skills

Body Opponent Bag Combinations

- Non-telegraphic movement
- Muscular relaxation

Fighting attributes are not just limited to the physical plane, there are mental and psychological fighting attributes that can be developed through consistent BOB training. They can include:

- Confidence
- Mental concentration
- Aggressiveness
- Psychological resilience

Stress Reduction

There's no escaping the fact that mental stress can do a tremendous amount of damage by causing heart disease, high blood pressure, chest pain, and an irregular heartbeat. It's no wonder stress is called the "silent killer."

The good news is; working out on the BOB regularly can be an excellent form of stress reduction. Punching and kicking an inanimate object, such as the body opponent bag, permits you to channel pent-up aggression in a productive fashion.

Cardiovascular Conditioning

If you workout on the body opponent bag with a significant amount of intensity, you can turn it into a cardiovascular workout. However, this will require you to really move around the bag and throw your punches, kicks and strikes at a respectable pace. Keep in mind, if you deliver your blows and strikes with full power and intensity, your workout will quickly become an anaerobic workout and you will most likely fizzle out.

Body opponent bag sessions can last anywhere from 30 seconds to 5 minutes depending on your level of conditioning, personal goals and training objectives.

Improving Muscle Tone

Body opponent bag training can also improve the muscle tone in your entire body including your back, chest, shoulders, arms, chest, abs, legs and calves. A typical workout can also burn a significant amount of calories and therefore can be a good method for stripping fat from the body.

Anger Management Tool

Unless you live on your own island, you will most likely live in a populated region that puts you in contact with many people everyday. Add a hectic lifestyle to the mix and you will most likely have conflicts with other people from time to time. This is when you will sometimes get the urge to respond in a "physical manner" but as a law abiding citizen you can't act on this and must repress these primitive urges.

Working out on the body opponent bag allows you to physically vent toxic anger in an acceptable and appropriate way. It's no wonder the bag is one of the most recommended items for children and adults in therapy.

"Punching and kicking an inanimate object, such as a body opponent bag, permits you to channel pent-up aggression in a productive fashion."

The BOB can also be used for developing your weapon skills. In this photo, the author strikes the body opponent bag with a kubotan mini stick.

Bob's Only Drawback...

There is only one drawback to the body opponent bag, and it's his head! As I mentioned earlier, the body opponent bag is ideal for punching accuracy, specialized self-defense training, open hand strikes, weapons training, choking techniques, etc. However, when it comes to throwing powerful knockout headshots, the body opponent bag does have some limitations.

More specifically, the head of the body opponent bag is relatively light and flexible and cannot withstand the effect of power punching. The bottom line, it just doesn't offer the resistance necessary for powerful heavy hitters. However, that's not to say that you can't get a great workout, you can! Just understand that it does have limitations.

As a matter of fact, the torso of the body opponent bag provides tremendous resistance against powerful body shots and will give the most seasoned fighter a fantastic workout.

Pictured here, the author demonstrates what happens when you deliver a powerful head shot on the Body Opponent Bag. Notice how the head of the bag can't resist the impact of the blow.

Chapter 2
BOB Set Up & Equipment

Body Opponent Bag Combinations

Finding The Right Location to Train

One important considerations when setting up the body opponent bag is finding the right location for training. First, you will need a place that will allow you to move around the bag. The location you choose should be a quiet place that is free from distractions. Here are a few locations you might want to consider when setting up your bag:

- Garage
- Carport
- Basement
- Barn
- Home gym (if you are fortunate enough)
- Warehouse
- Under a Deck

The of the greatest benefits of owning a BOB is that you don't have to deal with the daunting issues of installing a heavy bag mounting system. For example, if you owned a traditional heavy bag, you would have to find a beam to hang the bag or install a mount hanger into the wall stud.

Filling Up the Base of the Bag

Once you find the ideal location for training, the next task is filling the body opponent bag. Essentially, you have one of three options when filling the base. They are:

- **Water**
- **Sand**
- **Gravel**

If you plan on using a dry weight material perform the following steps: Unscrew the cap located on the top of the base, insert a funnel into the hole and carefully pour the material into the base. When the base appears full, secure the cap and tilt the base side to side to evenly distribute the material. Continue refilling the material if necessary.

If you are using water to fill the base perform the following. Unscrew the cap, insert a water hose into the hole and fill the base within two inches of the threaded inlet. Replace the cap. Important: After using the BOB a few times, unscrew the cap and let any air pressure escape from the base.

Setting the Proper Height

Now it's time to set the proper height of the body opponent bag. This is especially important for people who intend on using the BOB for self-defense or sport combat competition like mixed martial arts. For all practical purposes, the top of the BOB should be approximately head level with you. This will ensure that your targets are realistic.

Adjusting the height of the BOB is easy. In fact, the base of the body opponent bag allows you to adjust the height of the mannequin to seven different positions, each one in three-inch increments.

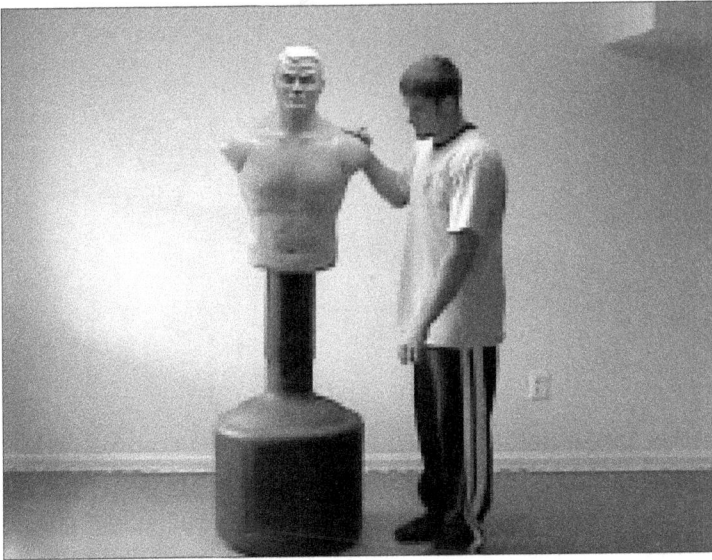

Not to tall and not too short. Pictured here, the ideal height for BOB training.

Begin by placing the torso of the BOB on the stem of the base. This is accomplished by aligning the lock pins (inside the torso) with the channels on the stem. Once properly aligned, the torso should slide effortlessly down the stem and to the base.

To change the hight of the bag, perform the following:

1. Align the lock pins with the stem channel and slide the torso upwards three inches at a time until it reaches the desired height.

2. Next, twist the torso of the mannequin until the lock pins slide to the ends of the channel and fall into place.

Body Opponent Bag Combinations

The stem of the body opponent bag allows you to adjust the height of the bag to seven different positions, each one in three inch increments.

You can adjust the torso of the mannequin to meet your personal workout preference. In this photo, the author prepares to fight a much taller adversary.

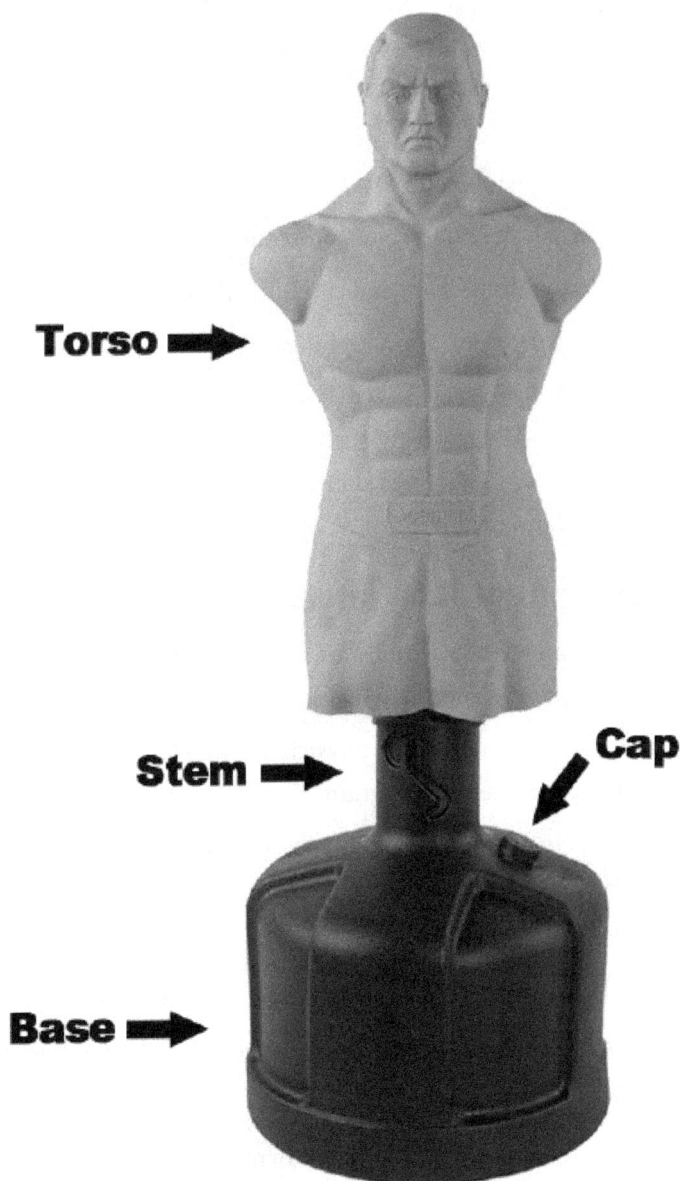

Torso ➡️

Stem ➡️

Cap ⬅️

Base ➡️

Moving the Body Opponent Bag

One of the greatest benefits of the body opponent bag is the ability to transport it quickly and easily. If you plan to move the body opponent bag a short distance, try the rolling technique. To perform this, do the following:

1. Remove the mannequin torso from the stem.

2. Make certain the cap is tight and secure.

3. Grab the top of the stem and carefully tilt the unit to you.

4. While in the tilt position, carefully roll the base to the desired location.

If you plan to relocate the BOB a greater distance, your best bet is to load it on a two-wheeled hand dolly. Important: Never attempt to lift a filled body opponent bag unit.

Body Opponent Bag Safety Tips

Before you launch ahead and start hitting the BOB, it's important to go over some important safety tips.

• Consult with your personal physician before beginning this or any other strenuous exercise program.

• Immediately stop training if you feel pain or discomfort.

• To avoid injuries, always begin your workout with a light round first.

• Never hold your breath when working out on the bag.

• Always remember to exhale when delivering a blow to the bag.

• Always keep your workout area clear of objects.

• While punching or kicking the BOB, make certain that no one is standing near the bag. This includes pets.

• When setting up the BOB always follow the manufacturer's

instructions.

- To avoid hyper-extending your arm, never strike the bag unless you are absolutely certain you will make contact.

- Always warm up with light stretching before working out on the bag.

- Never place your BOB directly next to a window.

- Before working out, always check and make certain the torso is securely seated in the stem channel.

- When working out on the body opponent bag, remember to keep both of your hands up always.

- Always wear loose fitting clothing when working out.

- To avoid injuring your hands and damaging your BOB, never workout with rings or jewelry on your hands.

- Never strike the BOB with full-force until you have mastered the proper punching body mechanics.

- To avoid spraining or breaking your wrists, never bend your wrists when punching the bag.

- Don't strike the BOB with bare knuckles until your hands are conditioned to withstand the impact.

- Get into the habit of timing your rounds.

- Proper punching and kicking form is always more important than intensity.

- Never fully extend or "lock out" your arms when punching the bag.

- Depending on the type of punch or kick that you are executing, always maintain the correct distance from the bag.

- Never allow people to play or swing from the BOB.

- Avoid lifting your chin and exposing your centerline when

Body Opponent Bag Combinations

working out on the bag.

• Maintain proper footwork and stay balanced always when working out.

• If your hands are sore from a previous workout, consider wearing a pair of boxing gloves the next time you work out.

Body Opponent Bag Gear

If you want to get the most out of your workouts, you might want to invest in some gear. Here are a few items you might want to consider buying to help you with your training.

Bag Gloves

Bag gloves are lightweight gloves that offer excellent protection to your hands when working out on all types of punching bags.

Bag gloves are constructed of either top grain cowhide or durable vinyl. There are generally two styles of bag gloves that are sold on the market:

• **Mitt style gloves**
• **Finger style gloves**

Some mitt style bag gloves may also have a small mental bar sewn into the palm grip area to aid in fist stabilization. Bag glove sizes are usually small, medium, large and extra large.

When buying bag gloves, spare no expense and look for a reputable and high quality brand. This will provide years of reliable use and will help ensure a better quality workout.

If you don't think you will need bag gloves, think again. Punching the body opponent bag without hand protection causes sore knuckles, bruised bones, hand inflammation, sore wrists and scraped knuckles. What is more important, it will set your training back for several weeks in order for your hands to heal.

Boxing Gloves

People often confuse bag gloves with boxing gloves. While the two might appear similar, they are quite different. Boxing gloves are heavier and significantly larger than bag gloves and they are generally used for full contact sparring sessions and sport combat competition.

However, boxing gloves also can be used for BOB training. In fact, advanced practitioners often use boxing gloves for developing

Body Opponent Bag Combinations

strength and endurance in their arms.

The ideal boxing glove is one that provides comfort, protection, and durability. Depending on your training objectives, the glove can weigh anywhere from ten to sixteen ounces.

Here are some important features to be aware of when buying a pair of boxing gloves:

• To avoid wrist injuries, you want the glove to fit snugly around your hand.

• The boxing glove should be composed of multi layered foam padding.

• The glove should have a sufficient palm grip that provides comfort and fist stabilization.

• To avoid a thumb injury, the glove should have thumb-lock stitching.

• The glove should be double-stitched to ensure durability.

• The entire glove should be constructed of top quality materials to increase its durability.

• The glove should be easy to slip-on and off your hands. Velcro fasteners are preferred over laces.

Hand Wraps

Hand Wraps are used by experienced athletes who want an added measure of protection to their hands when hitting the bag. They provide support for the entire hand and wrist area and can help prevent osteoarthritis in later years.

Essentially, hand wraps are long strips of cloth measuring two inches wide and nine to eighteen feet long. Longer hand wraps are used by practitioners who have large hands and who wish to have greater hand protection. You can find hand wraps at most sporting goods stores as well as the Internet.

Hand wraps should only be used in conjunction with either large bag gloves or boxing gloves, do not strike the bag with just your hand

Body Opponent Bag Combinations

wraps as this can easily injure your hands.

Hand wraps are washable and should be cleaned after every workout. Although there is a wide range of hand wrapping techniques, the procedures shown on the next page is suggested.

While hand wraps are a necessary piece of training equipment for boxing, mixed martial arts and other competitive combat sports, I don't recommend using them for self-defense training.

Since body opponent bag training is structured around time and rounds, you should invest in a good workout timer. Workout timers are used by boxers, mixed martial artists, kick boxers, and fitness enthusiasts to keep track of their time during their rounds.

Most workout timers will allow you to adjust your round lengths anywhere from thirty seconds to nine minutes. Rest time can be adjusted from thirty seconds to five minutes depending on your level of conditioning and training goals.

There are a wide variety of timers that are sold on the market and they will vary in price. Your best bet is to search the Internet for a timer that meets your specific needs.

Workout Timers are great for:

• Keeping track of the number of rounds and the time of each round when working out alone.

• Measuring your current level of cardiovascular conditioning.

• Monitoring your progress in your training.

• Creating healthy competition in your workout routine.

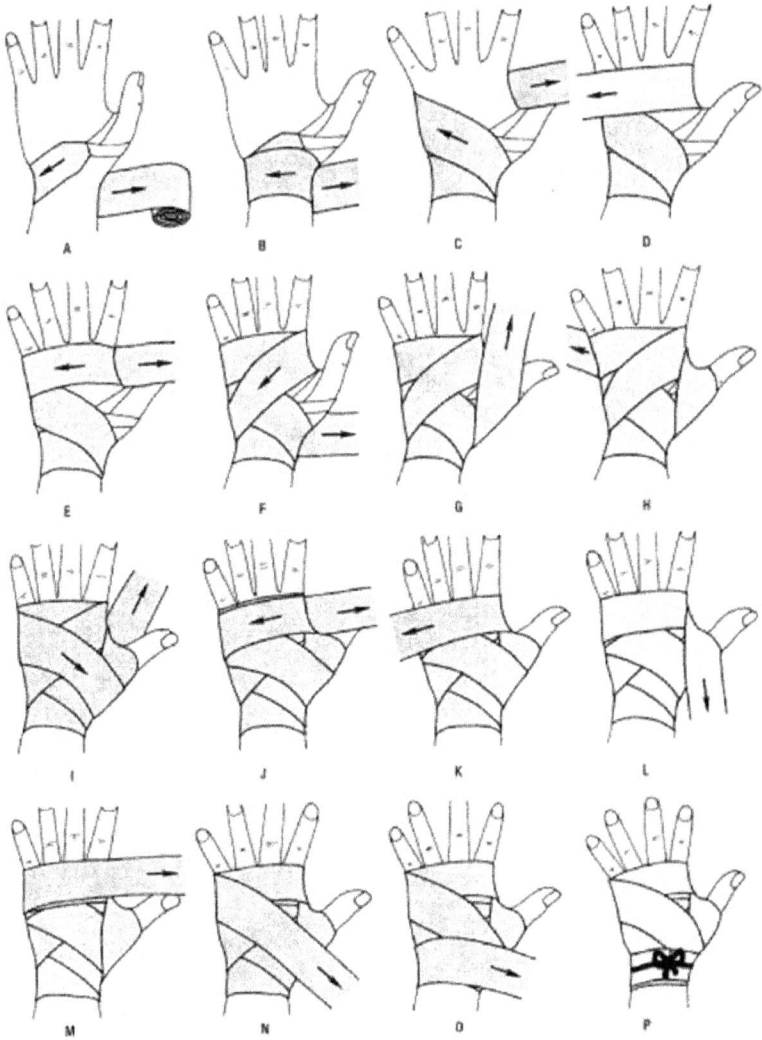

How to wrap your hands with hand wraps. Follow steps A through P.

Body Opponent Bag Combinations

Chapter 3
Targets and Techniques

Body Opponent Bag Combinations

Body Opponent Bag Targets

One of the greatest advantages of working out on the Body Opponent Bag is it's 360-degree targeting. If fact, one of the biggest mistakes you can make when training is to strictly hit the mannequin head on.

Since anatomically targets are located on all sides of the bag, you should take full advantage and move around it when training.

The targets featured in this chapter can be used for both self-defense and combat sports, such as boxing, mixed martial arts and kick boxing. With that being said, let's take a look at some of the Body Opponent Bag workout targets.

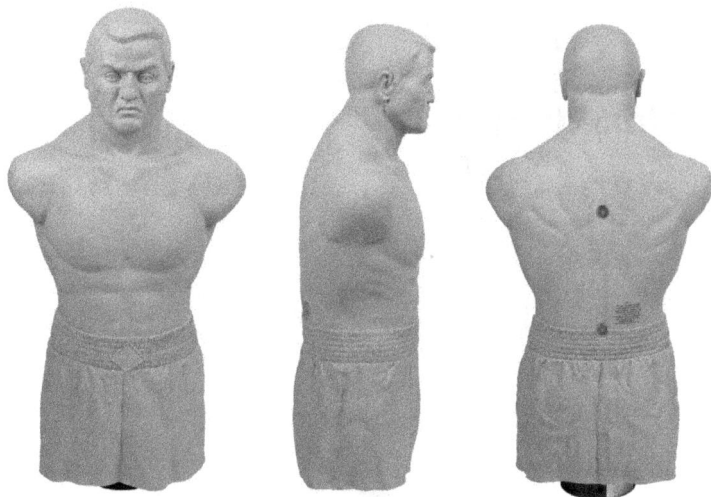

Anatomical targets are located all around the body opponent bag, so remember to move around it when working out.

Front Targets

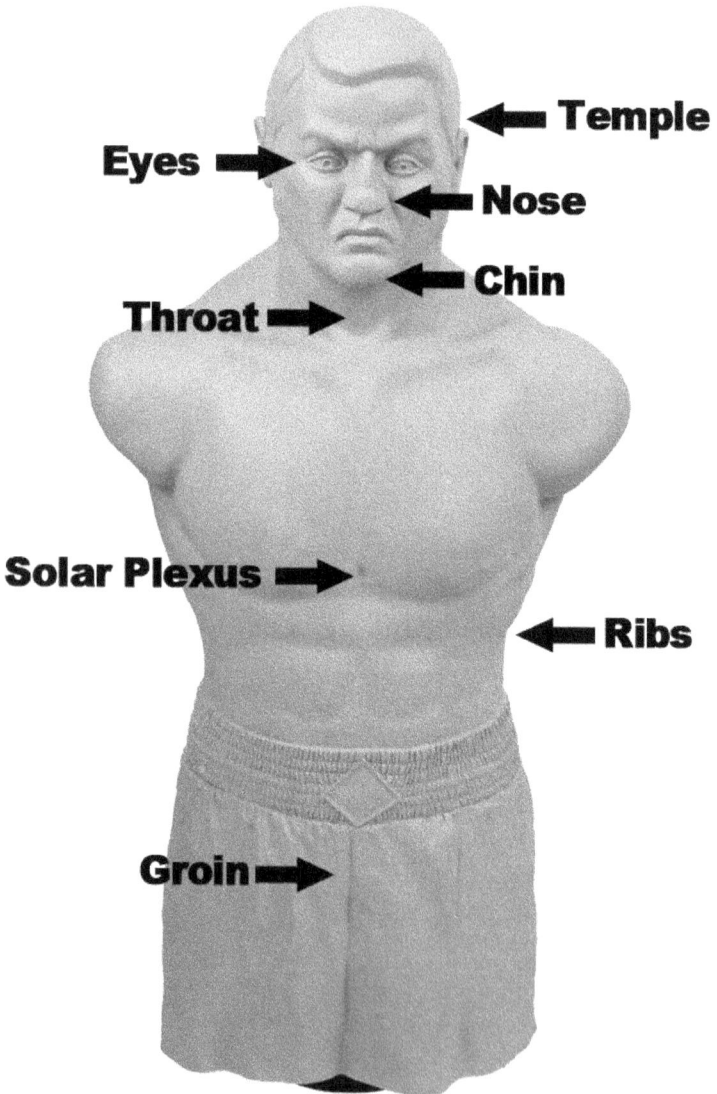

Temple

Eyes

Nose

Chin

Throat

Solar Plexus

Ribs

Groin

Rear Targets

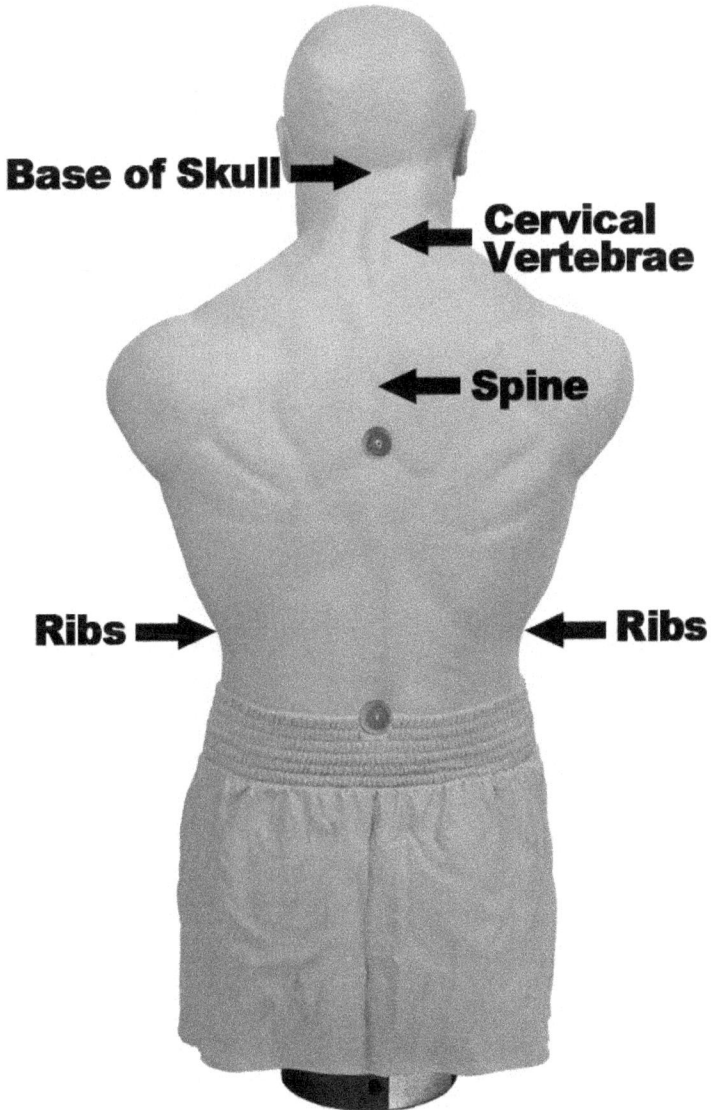

Base of Skull →

← **Cervical Vertebrae**

← **Spine**

Ribs →   ← **Ribs**

Side Targets

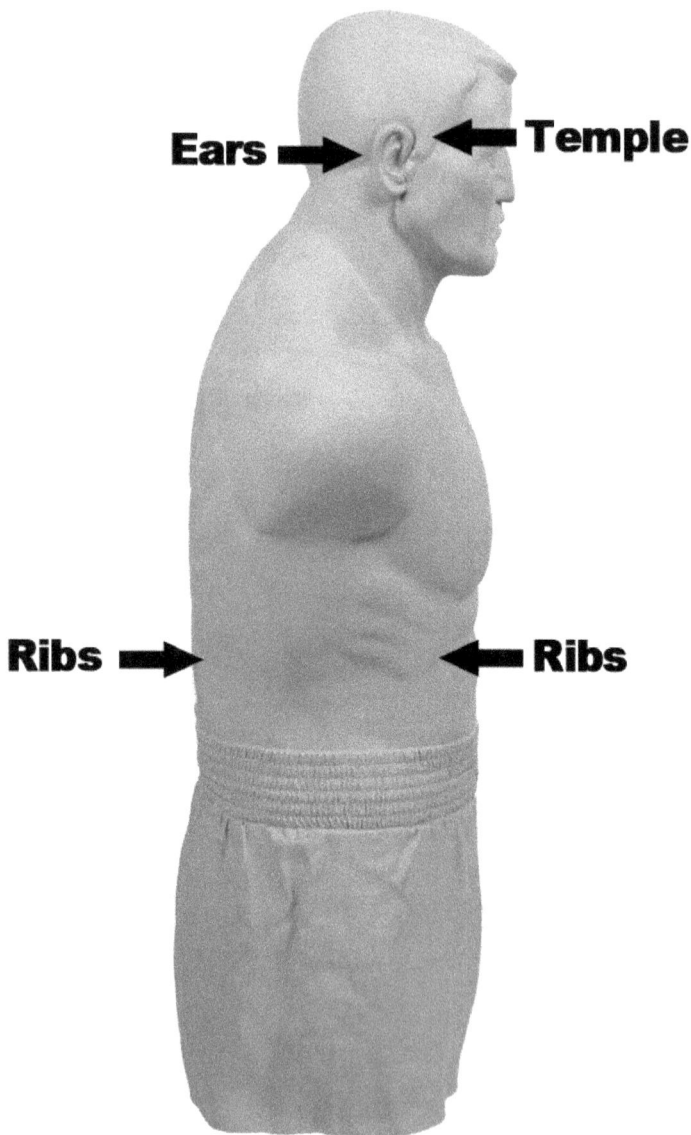

Ears ➡️ ⬅️ Temple

Ribs ➡️ ⬅️ Ribs

Foundational Fighting Skills

In this section, I am going to teach you the foundational techniques required to perform all of the Body Opponent Bag combinations featured in this book. These basic skills include the fighting stance, mobility and footwork, ranges of fighting, and various punching and striking techniques. Let's begin with the fighting stance.

The Fighting Stance

The fighting stance defines your ability to execute both offensive and defensive techniques, and it will play a material role in the outcome of a fight. It stresses strategic soundness and simplicity over complexity and style. The fighting stance also facilitates optimum execution of your body weapons while simultaneously protecting your vital targets against quick counter strikes.

The fighting stance is designed around the centerline. The centerline is an imaginary vertical line running through the center of the body, from the top of your head to the bottom of the groin. Most of your vital targets are situated along this line, including the head, throat, solar plexus, and groin. Obviously, you want to avoid directly exposing your

Pictured here, a left lead fighting stance.

Body Opponent Bag Combinations

centerline to the assailant. To achieve this, position your feet and body at a 45-degree angle from the opponent. This moves your body targets back and away from direct strikes but leaves you strategically positioned to attack.

Many people make the costly mistake of stepping forward to assume a fighting stance. Do not do this! This action only moves you closer to your assailant before your protective structure is soundly established. Moving closer to your assailant also dramatically reduces your defensive reaction time. So get into the habit of stepping backward to assume your stance. Practice this daily until it becomes a natural and economical movement.

How to Assume a Fighting Stance

When assuming your fighting stance, place your feet about shoulder width apart. Keep your knees bent and flexible. Think of your legs as power springs to launch you through the ranges of fighting.

Mobility is also important, as we'll discuss it in a moment. All footwork and strategic movement should be performed on the balls of your feet. Your weight distribution is also an important factor. Since combat is dynamic, your weight distribution will frequently change. However, when stationary, keep 50 percent of your body weight on each leg and always be in control of it.

The hands are aligned one behind the other along your centerline. The lead arm is held high and bent at approximately 90 degrees. The rear arm is kept back by the chin. Arranged this way, the hands not only protect the upper centerline but also allow quick deployment of your body weapons. When holding your guard, do not tighten your shoulder or arm muscles prior to striking. Stay relaxed and loose. Finally, keep your chin slightly angled down. This diminishes target size and reduces the likelihood of a paralyzing blow to your chin or a lethal strike to your throat.

The best method for practicing your fighting stance is in front of a full-length mirror. Place the mirror in an area that allows sufficient room for movement; a garage or basement is perfect. Stand in front of the mirror, far enough away to see your entire body. Stand naturally with your arms relaxed at your sides. Now close your eyes and quickly assume your fighting stance. Open your eyes and check for flaws. Look for low hand guards, improper foot positioning or body angle, rigid shoulders and knees, etc.

Drill this way repeatedly, working from both the right and left side. Practice this until your fighting stance becomes second nature.

Footwork & Mobility

Now, that we have the fighting stance covered, it's time to talk about mobility and footwork. One common mistake beginners make is simply standing in front of the Body Opponent Bag and beating it to death. While this methodology might have some street fighting applications, it should not be your sole method of training on the BOB.

When working out on the BOB, you must integrate mobility with your punching combinations. This means that you will need to learn some of the basics of footwork.

I define mobility as the ability to move your body quickly and freely, which is accomplished through basic footwork. The safest footwork involves quick, economical steps performed on the balls of your feet, while you remain relaxed and balanced. Keep in mind that balance is your most important consideration.

Basic footwork can be used for both offensive and defensive purposes, and it is structured around four general directions: forward, backward, right, and left. However, always remember this footwork rule of thumb: *Always move the foot closest to the direction you want to go first, and let the other foot follow an equal distance.* This prevents cross-stepping, which can cost you your life in a high-risk combat situation.

Basic Footwork Movements

1. Moving forward (advance)- from your fighting stance, first move your front foot forward (approximately 12 inches) and then move your rear foot an equal distance.

2. Moving backward (retreat) - from your fighting stance, first move your rear foot backward (approximately 12 inches) and then move your front foot an equal distance.

3. Moving right (sidestep right) - from your fighting stance, first move your right foot to the right (approximately 12 inches) and then move your left foot an equal distance.

4. Moving left (sidestep left) - from your fighting stance, first move your left foot to the left (approximately 12 inches) and then move your right foot an equal distance.

Practice these four movements for 10 to 15 minutes a day in front of a full-length mirror. In a couple weeks, your footwork should be quick, balanced, and natural.

Circling Around the Body Opponent Bag

Since Body Opponent Bag training will require you to circle around it, you must know advanced footwork that requires you to circle your body around the bag. This is known as strategic circling.

Strategic circling is an advanced form of footwork where you will use your front leg as a pivot point. This type of movement can also be used defensively to evade an overwhelming assault or to strike the opponent from various strategic angles. Strategic circling can be performed from either a left or right stance.

Circling left (from a left stance) - this means you'll be moving your body around the opponent in a clockwise direction. From a left stance, step 8 to 12 inches to the left with your left foot, then use your left leg as a pivot point and wheel your entire rear leg to the left until the correct stance and positioning is acquired.

Circling right (from a right stance) - from a right stance, step 8 to 12 inches to the right with your right foot, then use your right leg as a pivot point and wheel your entire rear leg to the right until the correct stance and positioning is acquired.

Avoid Cross-Stepping When Hitting The Bag

Cross-stepping is the process of crossing one foot in front or behind the other when moving around the bag. Such sloppy footwork makes you vulnerable to a variety of problems. Some include:

- It severely compromises your balance.
- It restricts the offensive flow of punching.
- It limits quick and rapid footwork.
- It can lead to a sprained ankle.

As I said before, the best way to avoid cross-stepping is to follow the basic footwork rule of thumb of always moving the foot closest to the direction you want to go first, and letting the other foot follow an equal distance.

BOB Fighting Ranges and Techniques

Before we get into the specific body opponent bag striking techniques, you first need to understand that the distance and angle of the Body Opponent Bag will dictate which striking technique you can execute at any given moment.

Therefore, you must know about the three fighting ranges. They include: kicking, punching, and grappling range. Let's begin with the kicking range.

Kicking Range

The furthest distance from the Body Opponent Bag is kicking range. At this range you are usually too far away to punch the bag, so you would use your legs to make contact. Kicking range techniques are powerful and can give your legs a tremendous workout.

Important: If you are strictly interested in BOB training for boxing, you can skip this and focus exclusively on the next section of this chapter.

While there is a myriad of kicking techniques in the martial arts world, here's a list of some of the basic kicking techniques you can use on the bag:

- Push kick (front leg)
- Push kick (back leg)
- Side kick (front leg)
- Hook kick (front leg)
- Hook kick (back leg)

Push Kick (from the front leg)

1. To perform the kick, begin from an orthodox stance (left side forward).

2. While maintaining your balance, shift your weight onto your back leg and raise your front leg up (your front knee should be bent at approximately 90 degrees).

3. Next, thrust with your hips and drive the ball of your front foot into the bag.

4. After contact is made with the bag, quickly retract your leg to the starting position. Remember to always keep your hands up when performing kicking techniques.

When performing the push kick be certain to hit with the ball of your foot and not your toes. Striking the bag with your toes can easily lead to a severe injury.

Push Kick (from the rear leg)

1. To perform the kick, begin from an orthodox stance (left side forward).

2. While maintaining your balance, push your back foot off the ground and shift your weight to your front leg (your rear knee should be bent at approximately 90 degrees).

3. Next, thrust with your hips and drive the ball of your foot into the bag.

4. After contact is made with the bag, quickly retract your leg to the starting position. Again, make certain to make contact with the ball of your foot and not your toes.

Side Kick (from the front leg)

1. To perform the side kick, begin from an orthodox stance (left side facing the bag).

2. While maintaining your balance, lean back and shift your weight onto your rear leg while simultaneously pivoting your

body so your centerline is approximately 90 degrees from the bag.

3. Raise your front knee up and close to your body (this is called the "chamber" position).

4. Next, use your hips and thrust your front leg forcefully into the bag. Contact is made with the heel of your foot.

5. After contact is made with the bag, retract your leg to the starting position.

Hook kick (front leg)

1. To perform the hook kick from your front leg, begin from an orthodox stance (left side facing the bag).

2. While maintaining your balance, lean back slightly and shift your weight to your rear leg.

3. Simultaneously raise your front knee up and towards the bag.

4. Next, quickly twist your front hip and swing your lead leg forcefully into the bag. Your front knee should be slightly bent when contact is made with the target. Avoid snapping your knee when performing the kick. Contact should be made with either the dorsum of your foot or shin bone.

5. After contact is made with the bag, bring your leg back to the starting position.

Hook kick (rear leg)

1. To perform the hook kick from your rear leg, begin from an orthodox stance (left side facing the bag).

2. While maintaining your balance, push off the back foot and shift your weight forward.

3. Next, raise your rear knee up and twist your hips forward as

you swing your rear leg forcefully into the bag.

4. Your rear knee should be slightly bent when impact is made with the bag. Avoid snapping your knee when performing the hook kick.

5. Again, contact should be made with either the dorsum of your foot or shin bone.

6. After contact is made with the bag, bring your leg back to the starting position.

Punching Range

The next distance is punching range and it's the range that you will be delivering most of your Body Opponent Bag combinations. At this distance, you're close enough to the bag to strike it with your fists. Punching range techniques should be quick, efficient and they should be the foundation of your Body Opponent Bag arsenal.

While there's a long list of punching techniques that can be performed on the bag, we are going to stick to the basics. They

In this photo, the author squares off with the BOB at the punching range.

Body Opponent Bag Combinations

include the following techniques:

- Jab
- Straight Right
- Hook punch
- Uppercut punch

The Jab

The jab is a foundation technique for boxers and mixed martial artists. This punch is thrown from your front hand, and it has a quick snap when delivered.

1. Start off in a fighting stance with both of your hands held up in the guard position. Your fists should be lightly clenched with both of your elbows pointing to the ground.

2. To perform the punch, simultaneously step to the bag and twist your front waist and shoulder forward as you snap your front arm into the bag.

3. When delivering the punch, remember not to lock out your arm as this will have a "pushing effect" on the bag.

4. Quickly retract your arm back to the starting position.

5. One common mistake when throwing the jab is to let it deflect off to the side of the bag. Also, keep in mind that jabs can be delivered to the head (top of the bag) or the body (middle of the bag).

Straight Right

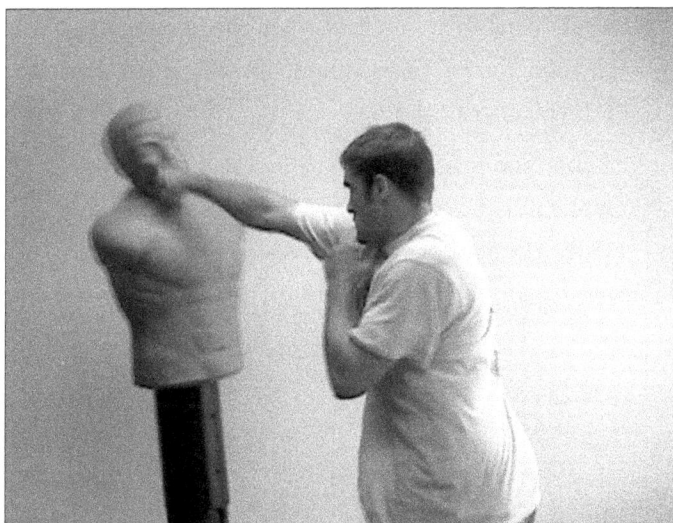

The straight right is considered the heavy artillery of linear punches. To execute the punch, perform the following steps:

1. Start off in a fighting stance with both of your hands held up in the guard position. Your fists should be lightly clenched with both of your elbows pointing to the ground.

2. To perform the punch, quickly twist your rear hips and shoulders forward as you snap your rear arm into the bag. Proper waist twisting and weight transfer is critical for the straight right. You must shift your weight from your rear foot

to your lead leg as you throw the punch.

3. To maximize the power of the punch, make certain that your fist is positioned horizontally. Avoid overextending the blow or exposing your chin during its execution.

4. Again, do not lock out your arm when throwing the punch. Let the power of the punch sink into the bag before you retract it back to the starting position.

When throwing liner punches, be certain not to lock your elbow. Elbow locking is a common problem among novices. There should always be a slight bend in your elbow when the punch hits the bag. Remember, if your elbow locks on impact, it will have a "pushing effect" and rob you of critical power.

Another common mistake when throwing the straight right on the body opponent bag is to let the punch glide downwards after contact is made. Always remember, the trajectory of initiating your punch must also be the very same trajectory of retracting your punch.

Hook Punch

The hook is another devastating punch in your arsenal of techniques, yet it's also one of the most difficult to master. This punch can be performed from your front or rear hand and it can be thrown high or low to the bag. There are two variations of the hook punch, they include:

- Traditional Hook Punch
- Modified Hook Punch

However, for the purpose of this book, I will teach you the traditional hook punch that is used in most boxing circles.

1. Start in a fighting stance with your hand guard held up. Both of your elbows should be pointing to the ground, and your fists should be loosely clenched.

2. To execute the hook punch, quickly and smoothly, raise your elbow up so that your arm is parallel to the ground while simultaneously torquing your shoulder, hip, and foot into the

direction of the blow.

3. When delivering the strike, be certain your arm is bent at least ninety degrees and that your wrist and forearm are kept straight throughout the movement.

4. As you throw the punch, your fist is positioned horizontally. The elbow should be locked when contact is made with the bag.

5. Return to the starting position.

6. Remember to simultaneously tighten your fists when they hit the bag. This action will allow your punch to travel with optimum speed and efficiency, and it will also augment the impact power of your strike.

In this photo, the author delivers a hook punch to BOB's ribs

Uppercut Punch

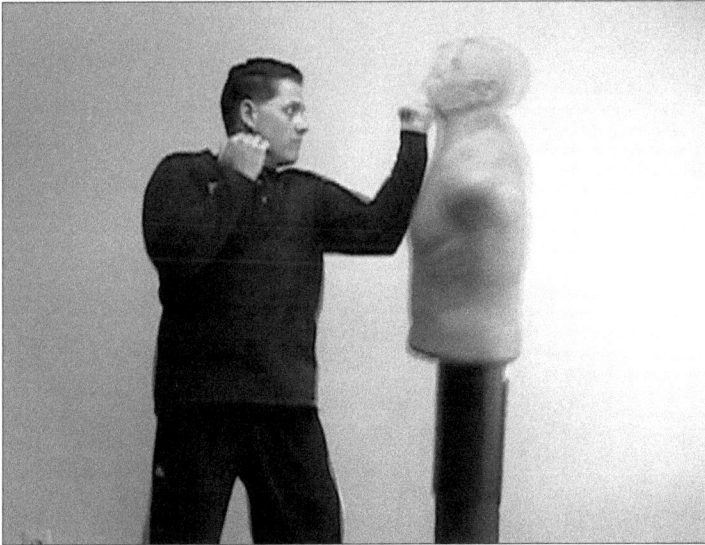

The uppercut is another powerful punch that can be delivered from both the lead and rear arm.

1. Start off in a fighting stance. Your fists should be lightly clenched with both of your elbows pointing to the ground.

2. To execute the uppercut, drop your shoulder, and bend your knees.

3. Quickly, stand up and drive your fist upward and into the bag. Your palm should be facing you when contact is made with the bag. To avoid any possible injury, keep your wrists straight.

4. Make certain that the punch has a tight arc and that you avoid all "winding up" motions. A properly executed uppercut should be a tight punch and should feel like an explosive jolt.

5. Return to the fighting stance.

Grappling Range

The third and closest range of fighting is grappling range. At this distance, you are too close to the bag to kick or execute linear punches (i.e., jab, straight right) so you would use close-quarter techniques.

Grappling range is divided into two different planes; vertical and horizontal. In the vertical plane, you would deliver impact techniques, some of which include elbow and knee strikes, head butts, gouging and crushing tactics, and biting and tearing techniques.

In the horizontal plane of grappling range, you are ground fighting with your opponent and can deliver all the previously mentioned techniques, including various submission holds, locks and chokes.

When it comes to body opponent bag training, grappling range striking techniques are going to appeal to three groups of people:

- Self-defense practitioners

- Mixed martial artists (MMA)
- Martial artists (traditional and eclectic)

You can add several grappling range techniques to your body opponent bag workout. Here are a few:

- Head butts
- Eye rakes
- Elbow strikes
- Neck cranks
- Knee strikes

Head Butt

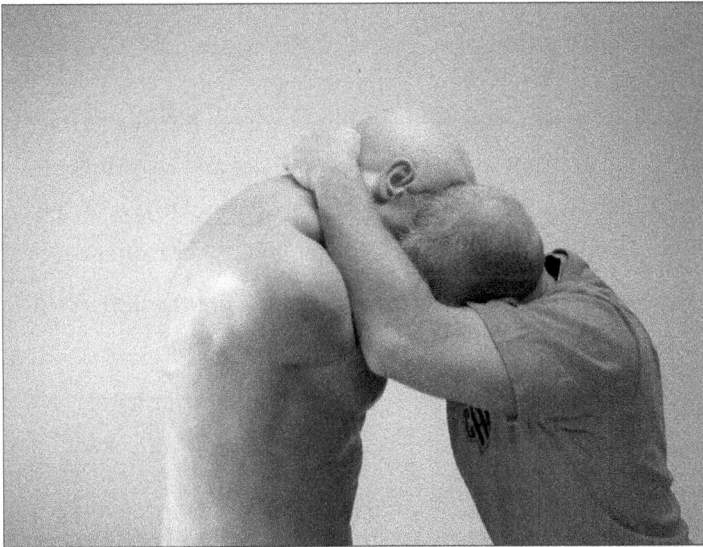

When squared off with the body opponent bag, you can deliver the head butt strike to his face. Head butts are ideal when a strong attacker has placed you in a hold where your arms are pinned against your sides. The head butt can be delivered in four different directions: (1) Forward; (2) Backward; (3) Right Side; (4) Left Side.

Horizontal Elbow

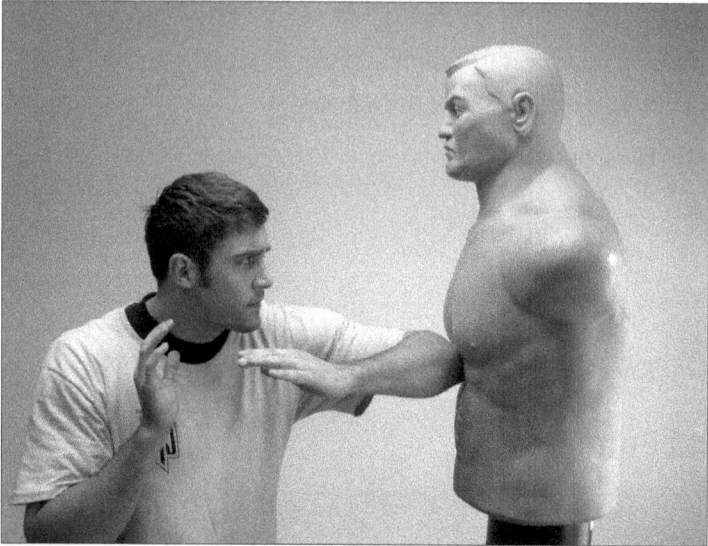

The elbows are devastating weapons that can be used in the grappling range. They are explosive, deceptive and very difficult to stop. Elbows can generally be delivered horizontally, vertically, diagonally and they can be thrown from either your front or rear arm.

Let's just take a look at the body mechanics of the horizontal elbow strike.

1. Start off in a fighting stance with both of your hands held up in the guard position. Make certain that you are standing in proximity to the bag.

2. To execute the elbow strike, quickly and smoothly, raise your elbow up so that your arm is parallel to the ground.

3. Next, simultaneously torquing your shoulder, hip, and foot into the direction of the bag. The tip of your elbow should reach the target.

4. Return to the starting position.

Diagonal Knee Strike

The knee strike is another devastating close-quarter grappling range tool that can do a lot of damage. The knee strike can also be delivered diagonally or vertically to the bag.

Here are the body mechanics of the diagonal knee strike.

1. To perform the diagonal knee strike from your rear leg, begin from an orthodox stance (left side facing the bag).

2. Next, grab hold of the bag with both hands.

3. While maintaining your balance, push off the back foot and shift your weight forward.

4. Next, raise your rear knee up and swing your hips and rear leg diagonally into the bag.

5. Your rear knee should be sharply bent when it hits the bag.

6. After contact is made, bring your leg back to the starting position.

Vertical Knee Strike

1. To perform the vertical knee strike from your rear leg, begin from an orthodox stance (left side facing the bag).

2. Next, grab hold of the bag with both hands.

3. While maintaining your balance, push off the back foot and shift your weight forward.

4. Next, raise your rear knee up and drive your hips and rear leg vertically into the bag.

5. Your rear knee should be sharply bent when impact is made with the bag.

6. After contact is made with the bag, bring your leg back to the starting position.

You can practice a wide variety of grappling and ground fighting skills on the body opponent bag. In this photo, the author perform the ground and pound technique.

Chapter 4
Beginner Combinations

Body Opponent Bag Combinations

Understanding Combination Punching

Since this book is devoted strictly to combinations, it's important for you to have a very clear understanding of its meaning.

A combination or "compound attack" is the logical sequence of two or more techniques thrown in strategic succession. For example, a jab followed by a straight right is considered to be a basic punching combination.

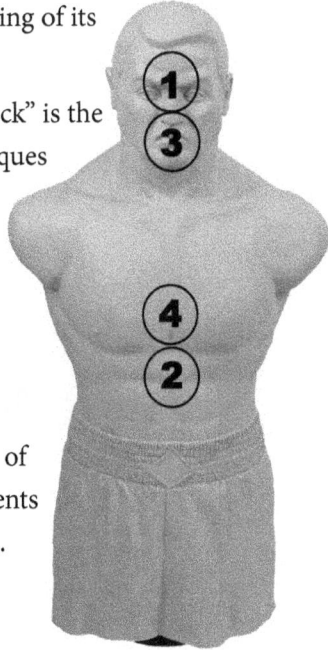

Unlimited Combinations

Besides the actual body mechanics of punching, there are several other elements that comprise a punching combination. They include attack rhythms, height variations, the cadence of delivery, and practitioner movement. Nevertheless, when you combine and manipulate all of these elements you truly have an infinite amount of punching combinations that you can perform on the Body Opponent Bag.

When reading the combination sequence on the following pages, please note the word "high" indicates punches delivered at head level while "low" represents punches delivered to the solar plexus or ribs on the bag.

Finally, for reasons of simplicity, all of the following punching combinations are demonstrated from a left lead stance.

Beginner Level Combinations

Combination #1: jab-jab (all high)

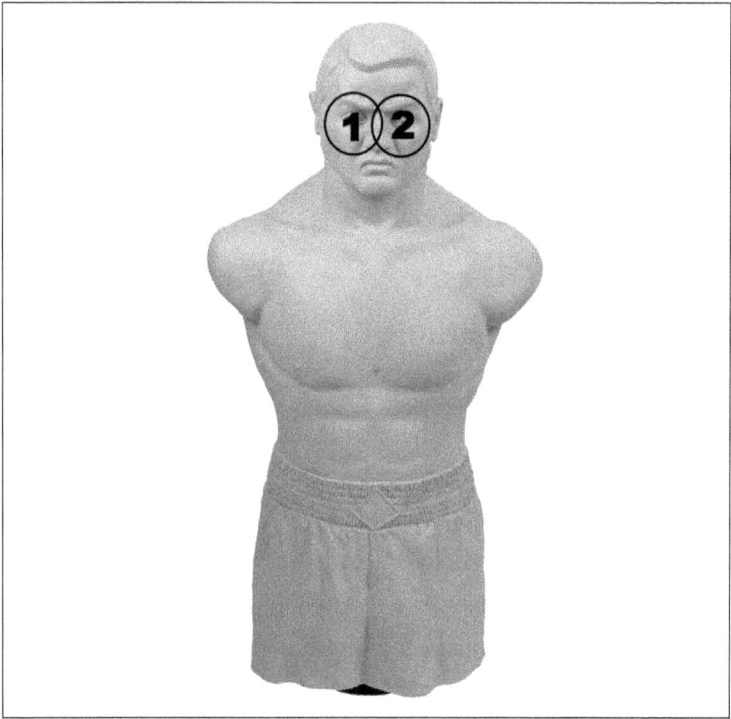

To perform the combination:

1. Extend your lead arm forward and jab high at the bag.

2. Jab again at the bag.

3. Return to a fighting stance.

Combination #2: jab-jab (all low)

To perform the combination:

1. From a fighting stance, bend your knees while snapping your lead arm at the solar plexus of the bag.

2. Follow up with another low jab.

3. Return to a fighting stance.

Combination #3: jab-jab (high-low)

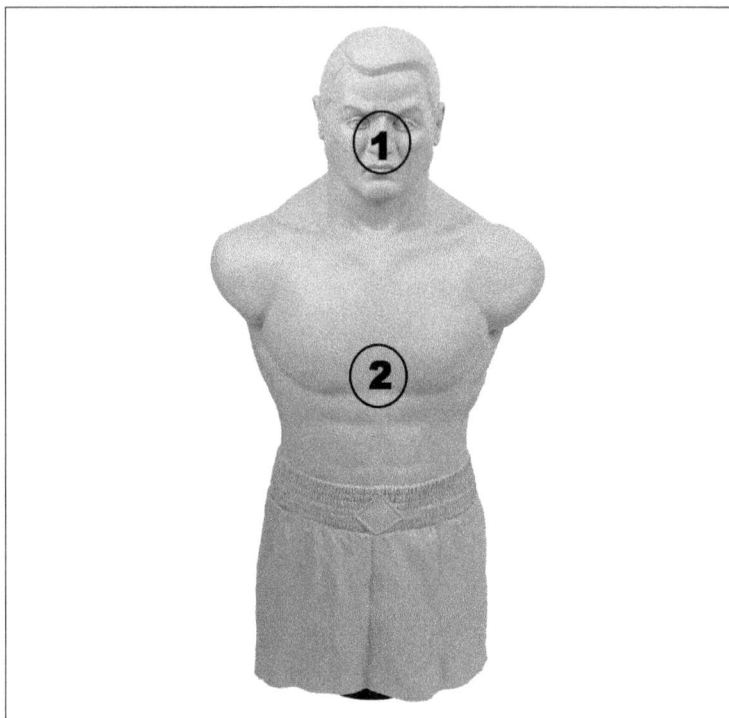

To perform the combination:

1. Jab high at the bag.

2. Return to a low stance position and jab low at the bag.

3. Return to your fighting stance.

Combination #4: jab-jab (low-high)

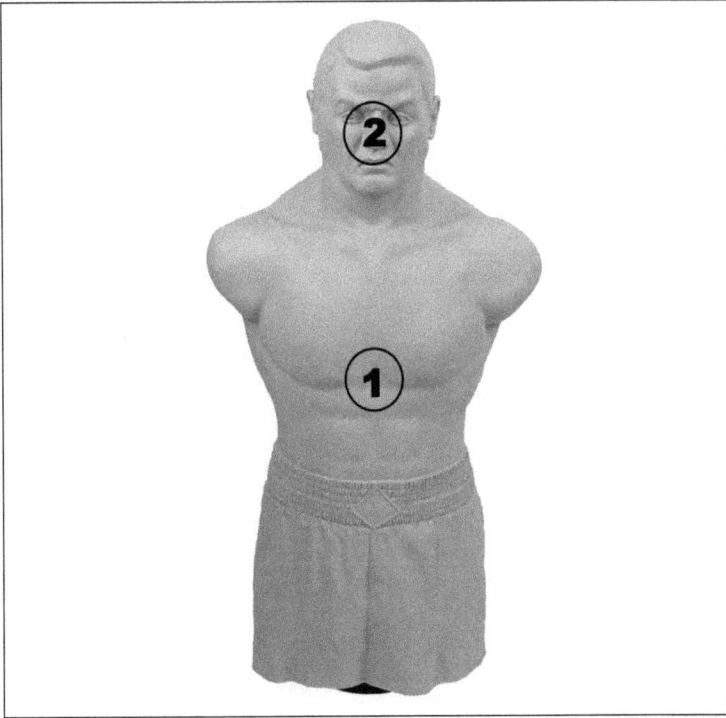

To perform the combination:

1. Bend your knees and jab low at the bag.

2. Quickly shoot up and jab high at the bag.

3. Return to a fighting stance.

Combination #5: jab-straight right (all high)

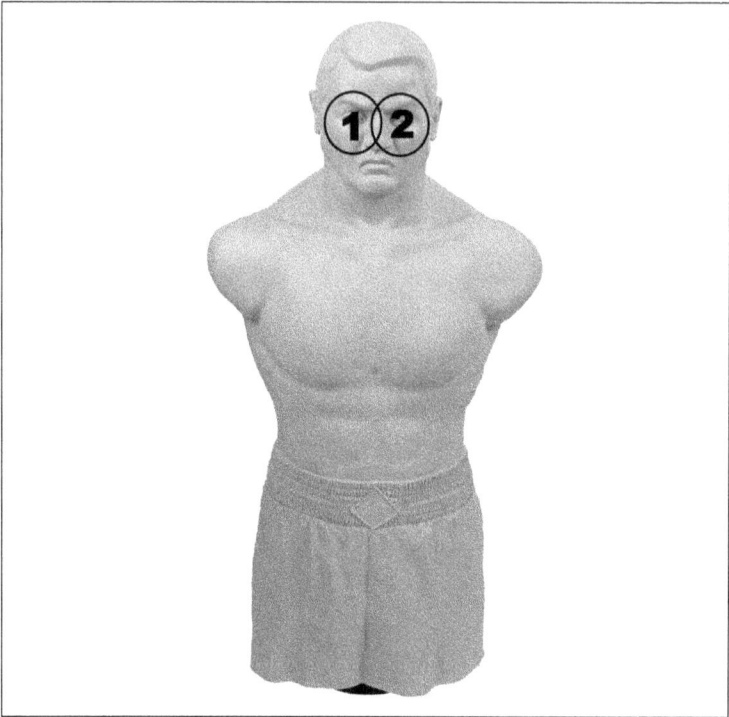

To perform the combination:

1. Extend your lead arm forward and jab high at the bag.

2. Next, deliver a straight right at the head.

3. Return to the stance position

Combination #6: jab-straight right (high-low)

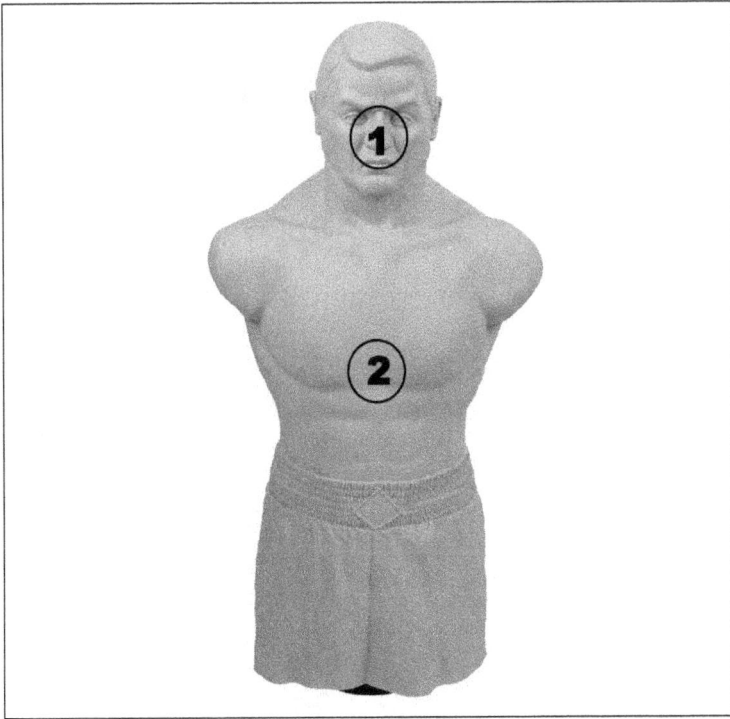

To perform the combination:

1. Jab high at the bag.

2. Next, deliver a straight right at the body.

3. Return to the stance position

Combination #7: straight right-jab (all high)

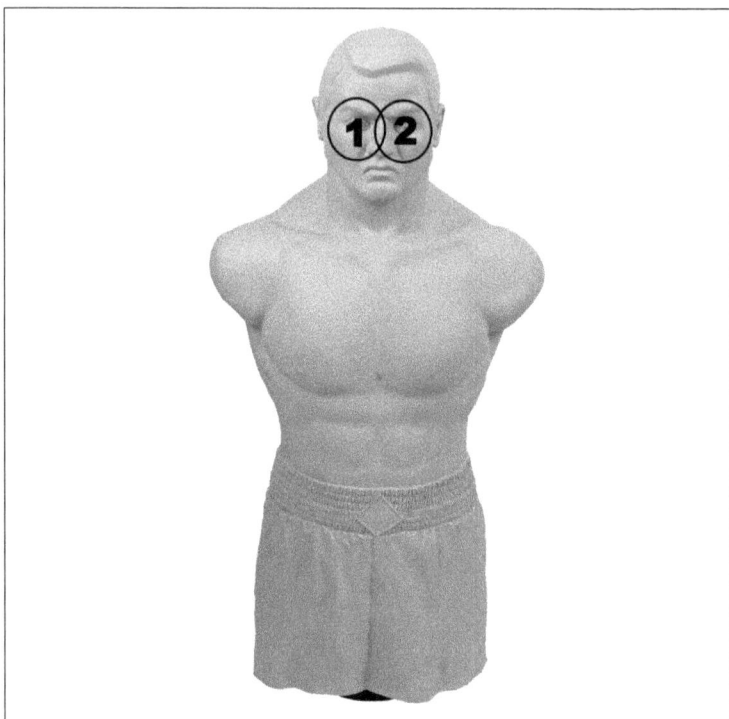

To perform the combination:

1. Deliver a high straight right.

2. Next, jab high at the bag.

3. Return to the stance position

Combination #8: jab-straight right-straight right (all high)

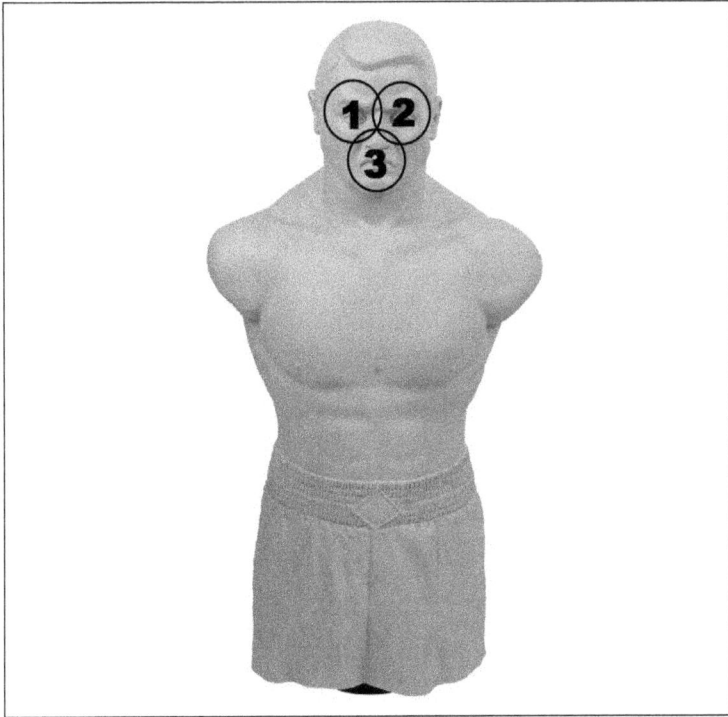

To perform the combination:

1. Jab high at the bag.

2. Next, deliver a high straight right.

3. Deliver another straight right.

4. Return to the stance position

Combination #9: straight right-jab-straight right-jab (all high)

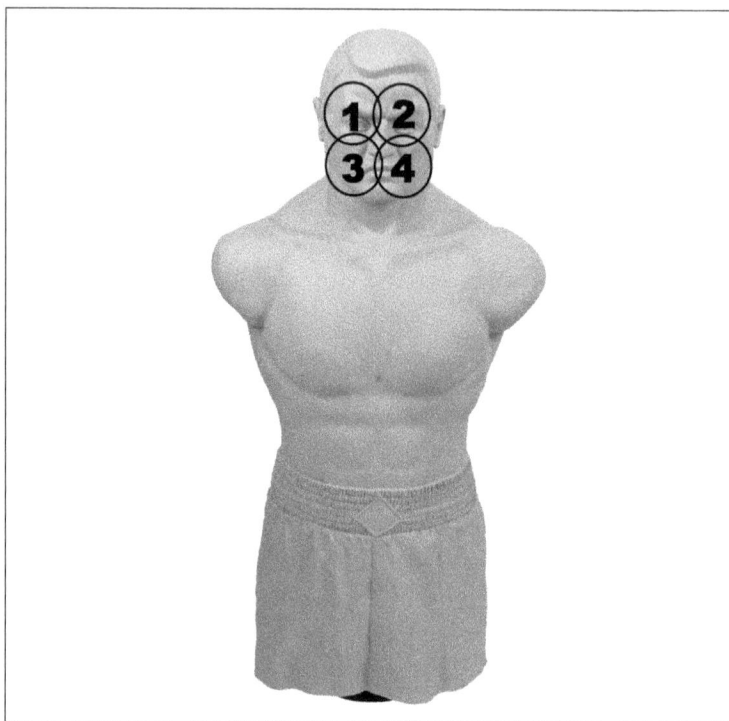

To perform the combination:

1. Deliver a high straight right to the bag.

2. Jab high at the bag.

3. Fire off a second high straight right.

4. Jab again at the bag.

5. Return to the stance position

Combination #10: jab-jab-straight right (all high)

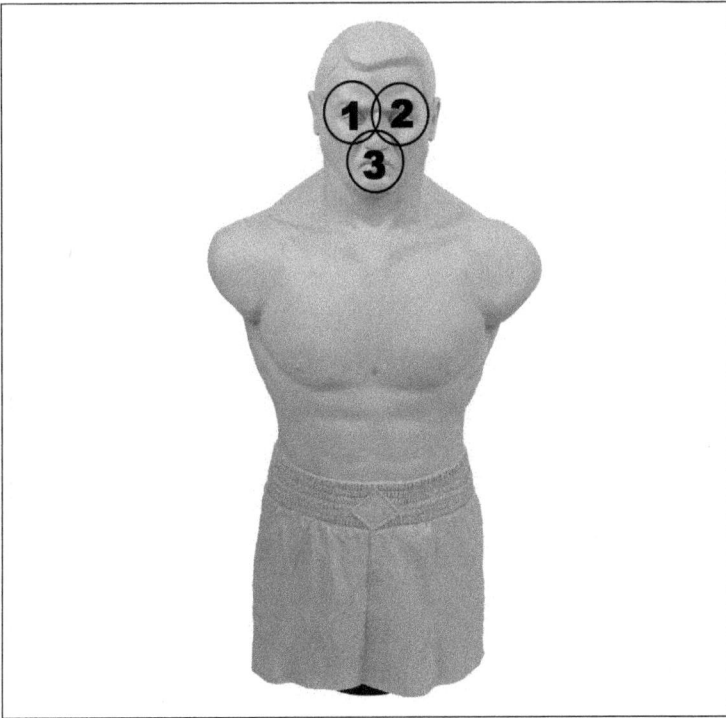

To perform the combination:

1. Jab high at the bag.

2. Fire off another high jab.

3. Next, follow up with a high straight right.

4. Return to the stance position

Combination #11: jab-jab-straight right (high-high-low)

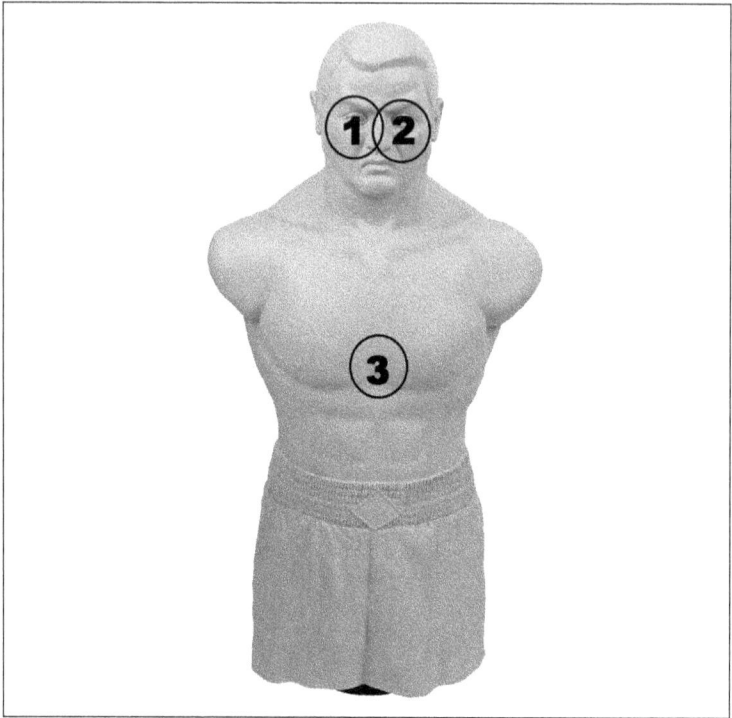

To perform the combination:

1. Jab high.
2. Fire off another high jab.
3. Next, follow up with a low straight right.
4. Return to the stance position

Combination #12: jab-straight right-jab (all high)

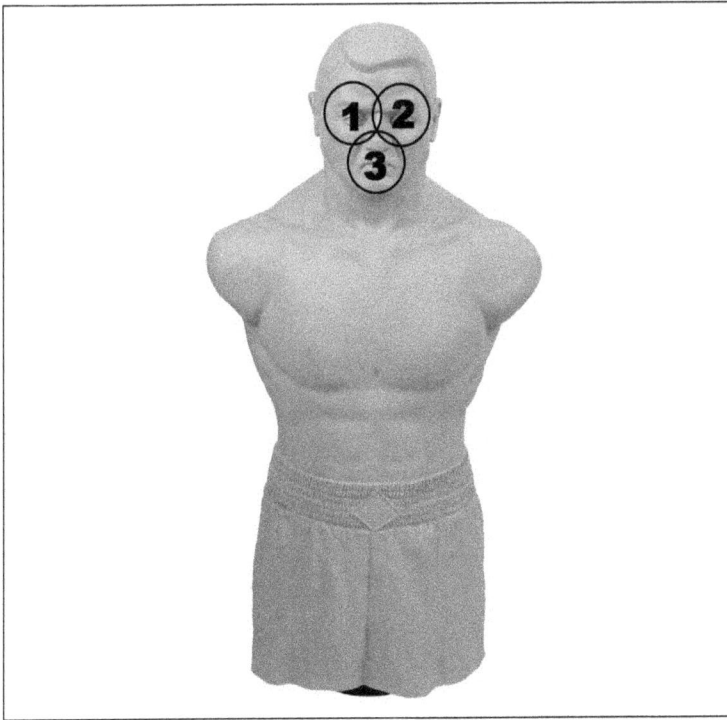

To perform the combination:

1. Jab high.
2. Next, throw a high straight right.
3. Follow up with another high jab.
4. Return to the stance position.

Combination #13: jab-straight right-jab (high-low-high)

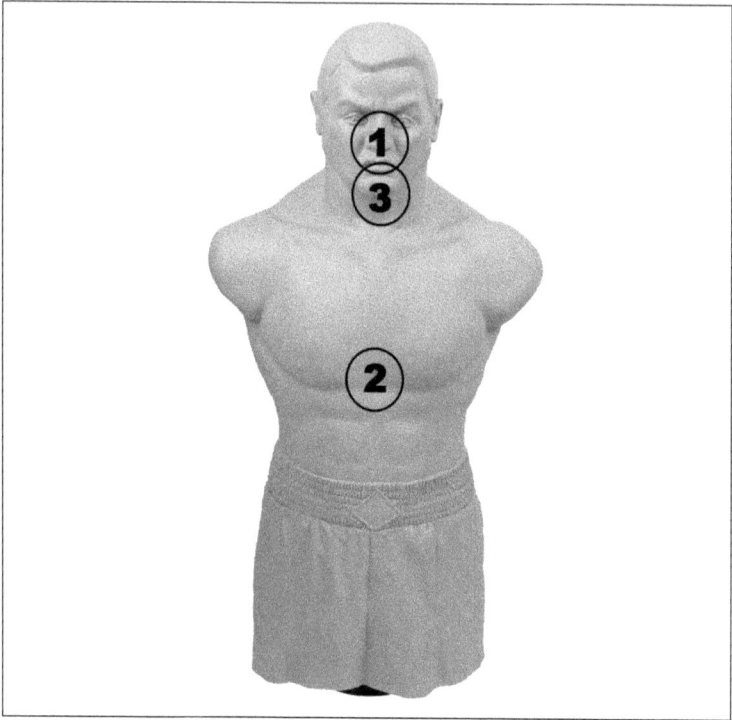

To perform the combination:

1. Jab high at the bag.

2. Next, throw a low straight right.

3. Follow up with another high jab.

4. Return to the stance position.

Combination #14: jab-straight right-jab-straight right (all high)

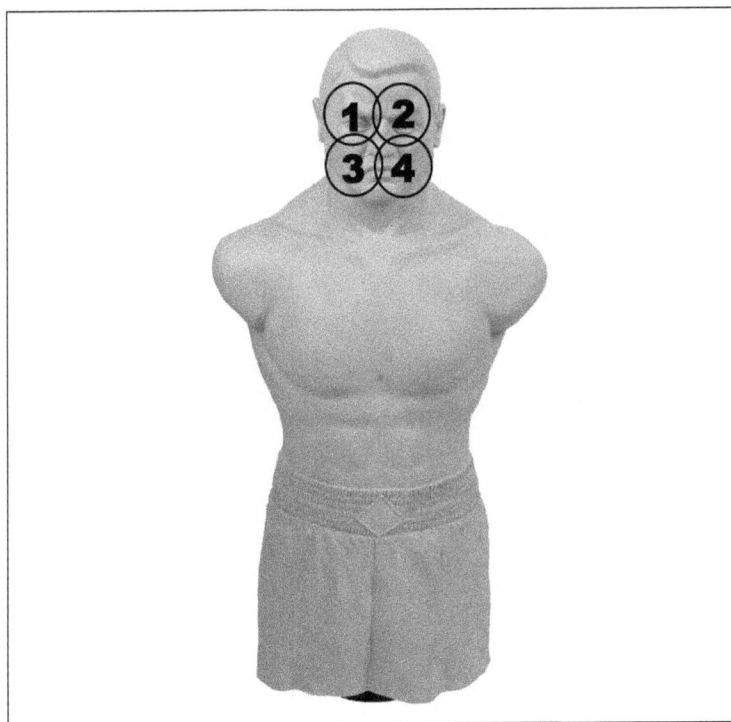

To perform the combination:

1. Jab high.

2. Next, throw a high straight right.

3. Follow up with another high jab.

4. Finish with another high straight right.

5. Return to the stance position.

Combination #15: jab-straight right-jab-straight right (high-low-high-low)

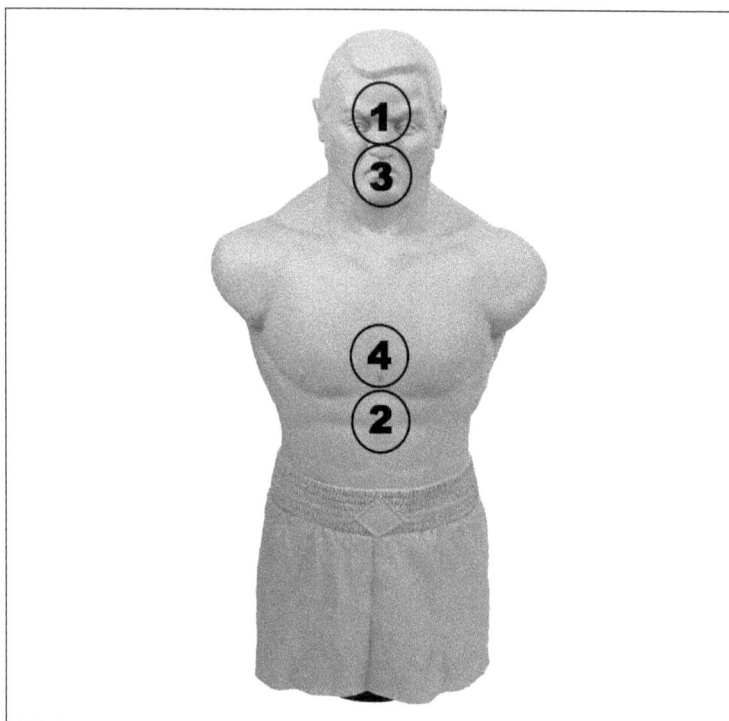

To perform the combination:

1. Jab high at the bag.
2. Next, deliver a low straight right.
3. Follow up with another high jab.
4. Finish with a low straight right.
5. Return to the stance position.

Combination #16: jab-straight right-jab-straight right (low-high-low-high)

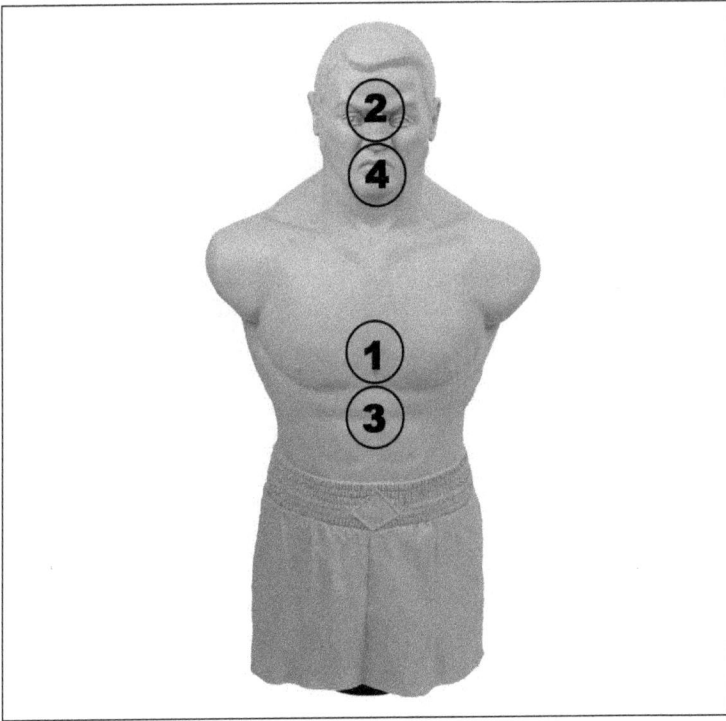

To perform the combination:

1. Jab low at the bag.

2. Next, throw a high straight right.

3. Follow up with another low jab.

4. Finish with a high straight right.

5. Return to the stance position.

Combination #17: jab-straight right-jab-straight right (all low)

To perform the combination:

1. Jab low at the bag.

2. Next, throw a low straight right.

3. Follow up with another low jab.

4. Finish with a low straight right.

5. Return to the stance position.

Combination #18: jab-jab-straight right (low-low-high)

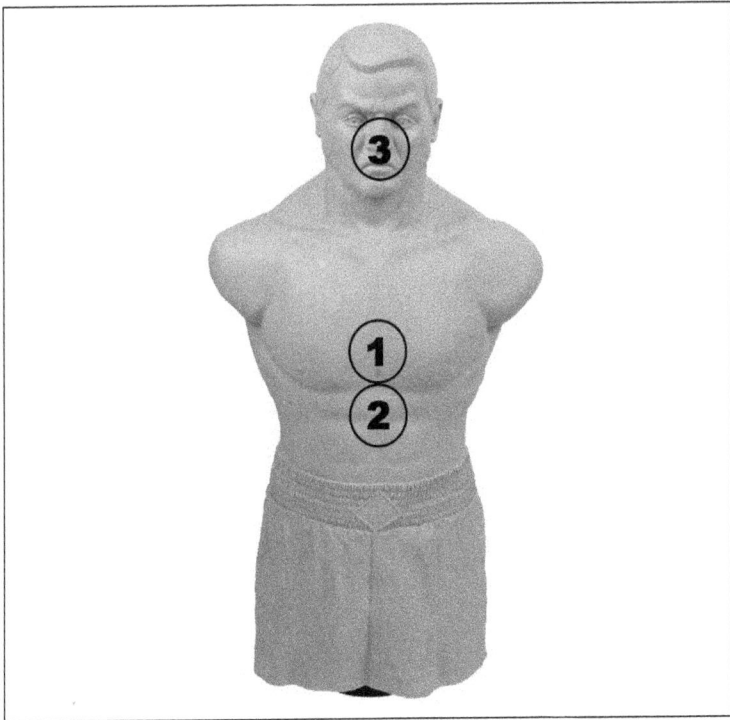

To perform the combination:

1. Jab low at the bag.

2. Next, throw another low jab.

3. Follow up with a high straight right.

4. Return to the stance position.

Combination #19: jab-jab-jab (high-low-high)

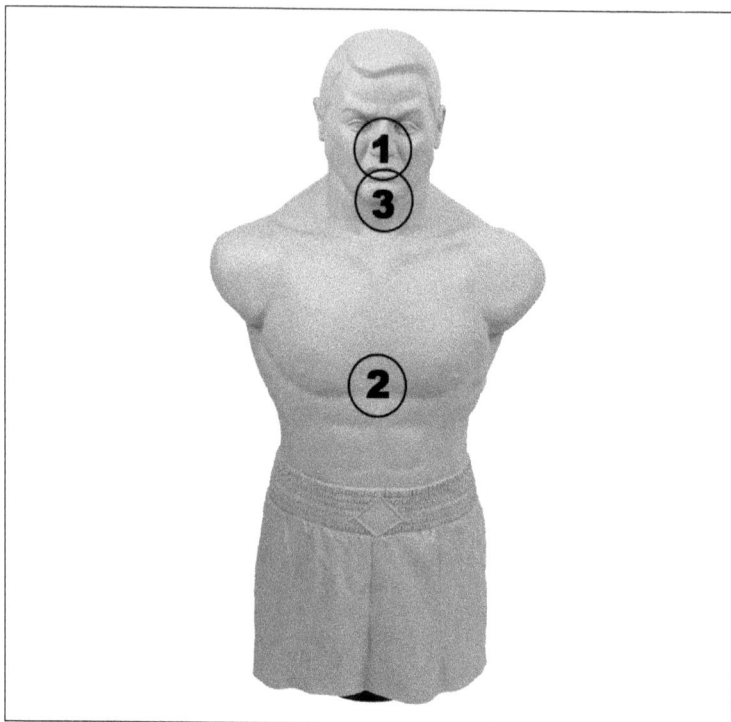

To perform the combination:

1. Jab high at the bag.

2. Next, deliver a low jab to the body.

3. Follow up with another high jab.

4. Return to the stance position.

Chapter 5
Intermediate Combinations

Body Opponent Bag Combinations

Adding Hooks to Your Combinations

In this chapter, we are going to build off the combinations from the previous chapter and add circular punches to your Body Opponent Bag workout. More specifically, you're going to add hook punches to your punching combinations.

The hook punch is a devastating blow delivered from both the lead and rear side of the body. However, it's also one of the most difficult to master.

To execute the hook punch correctly, you must maintain the correct wrist, forearm, and shoulder alignment. When delivering the punch, be sure your arm is bent at least 90 degrees and that your wrist and forearm are kept straight throughout the movement.

To execute the hook punch, quickly and smoothly raise your elbow up so that your arm is parallel to the ground while simultaneously torquing your shoulder, hip, and foot in the direction of the blow. Finally, avoid cocking the arm back or applying excessive follow-through.

Combination #20: jab-straight right-hook (all high)

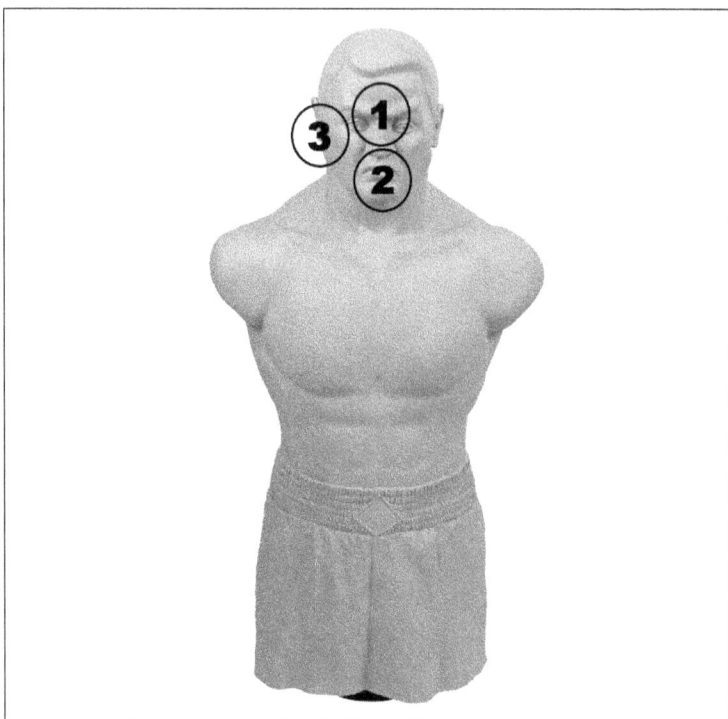

To perform the combination:

1. Jab high at the bag.

2. Next, deliver a high straight right to the bag.

3. Follow with a lead hook to the head.

4. Return to the fighting stance.

Combination #21: jab-straight right-hook (high-high-low)

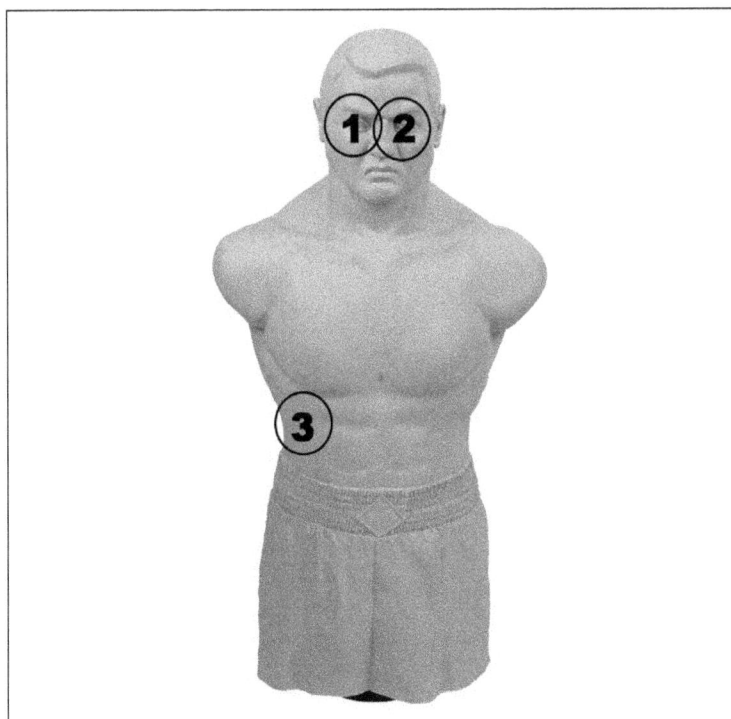

To perform the combination:

1. Jab high at the bag.

2. Next, deliver a high straight right to the bag.

3. Immediately follow with a lead hook to the body

4. Return to the fighting stance.

Combination #22: jab-straight right-hook-hook (all high)

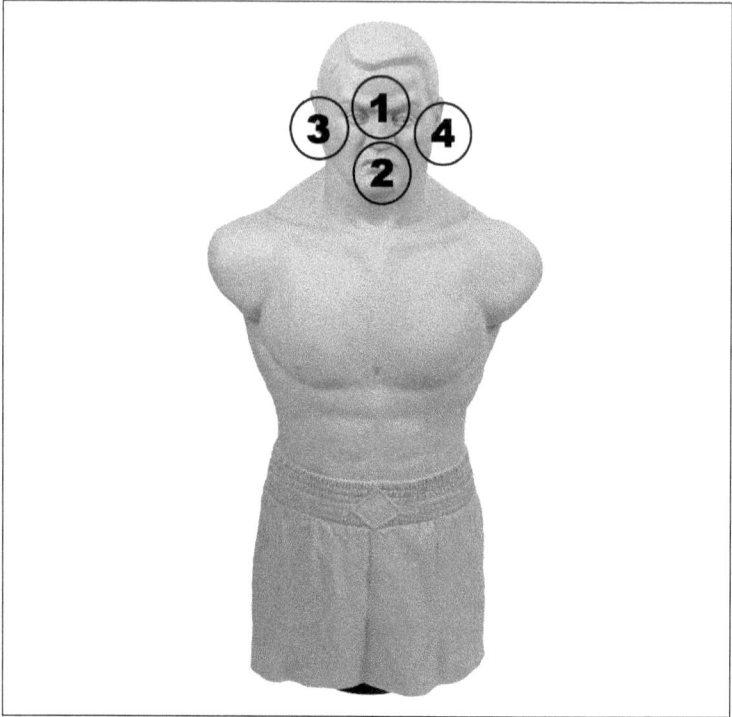

To perform the combination:

1. Jab high at the bag.

2. Deliver a high straight right.

3. Follow up with a lead hook to the head.

4. Next, deliver a high rear hook.

5. Return to the fighting stance.

Combination #23: jab-straight right-hook-hook (high-high-high-low)

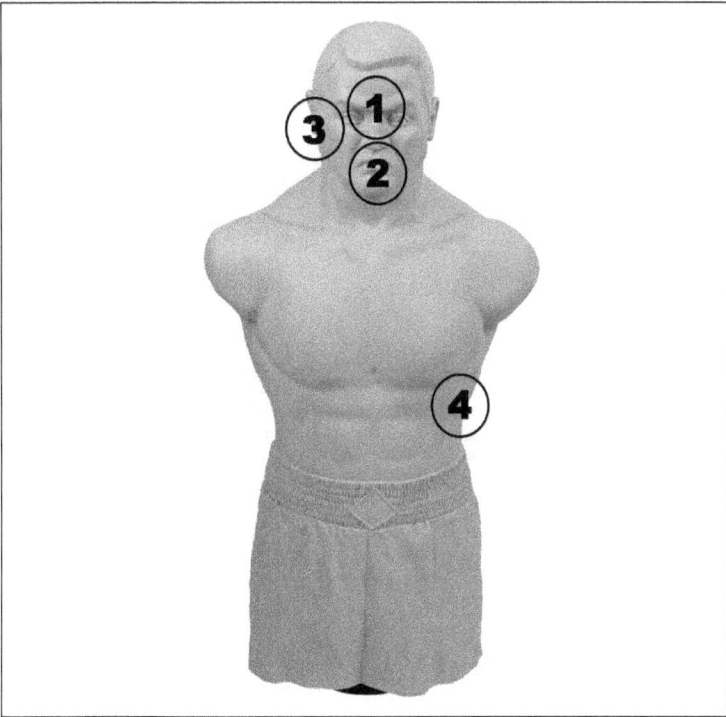

To perform the combination:

1. Jab high at the bag.

2. Deliver a high straight right.

3. Follow up with a lead hook to the head.

4. Next, deliver a low rear hook to the ribs.

5. Return to the fighting stance.

Combination #24: jab-straight right-hook-hook (high-high-low-high)

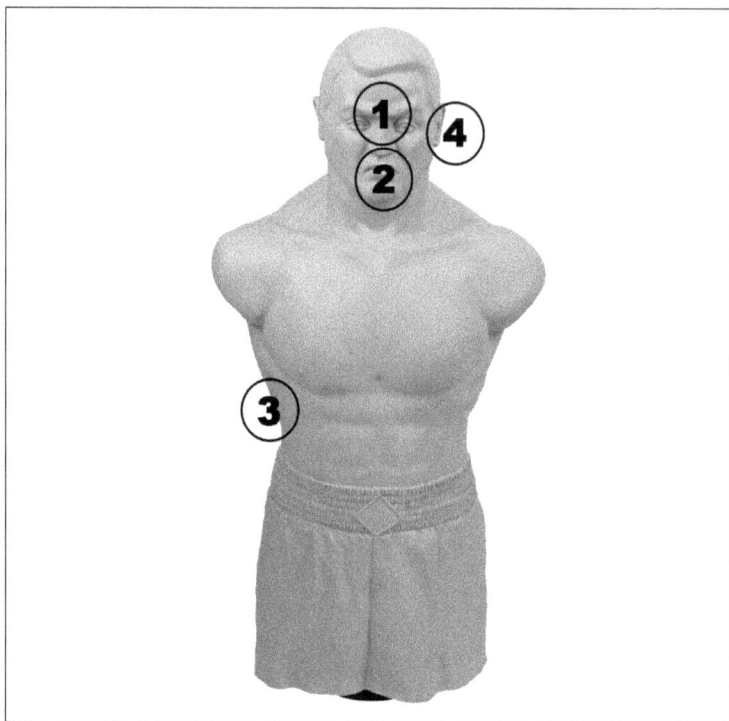

To perform the combination:

1. Jab high at the bag.

2. Deliver a high straight right.

3. Follow up with a lead hook to the ribs.

4. Next, deliver a high rear hook.

5. Return to the fighting stance.

Combination #25: jab-rear hook-rear hook (high-high-low)

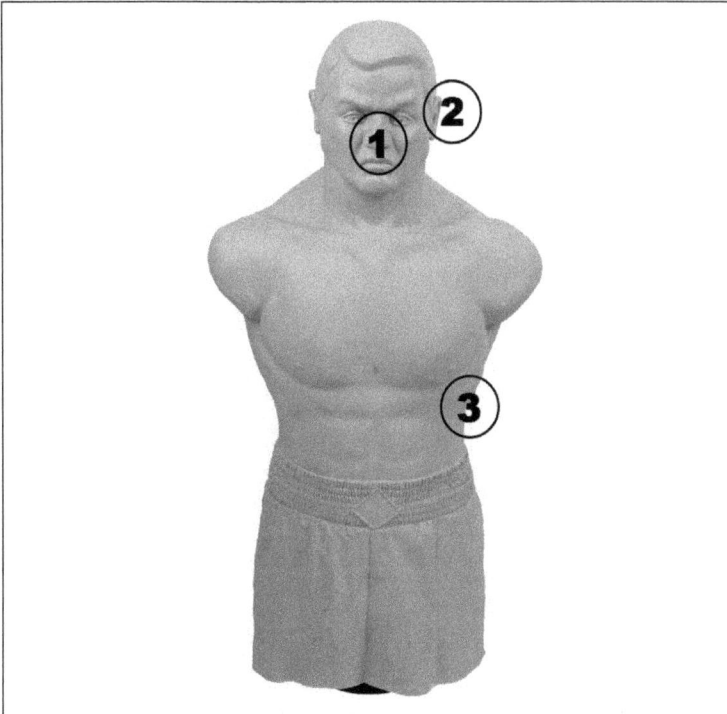

To perform the combination:

1. Jab high at the bag.

2. Next, deliver a rear hook to the head.

3. Follow with a rear hook to the ribs.

4. Return to the fighting stance.

Combination #26: jab-rear hook-rear hook (high-low-high)

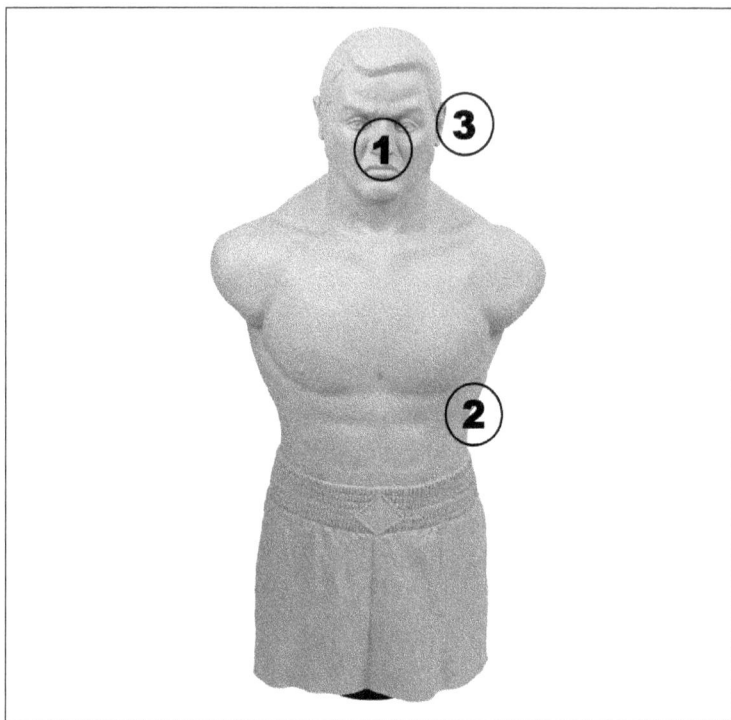

To perform the combination:

1. Jab high at the bag.

2. Next, deliver a rear hook to the ribs

3. Follow with a rear hook to the head.

4. Return to the fighting stance.

Combination #27: jab-lead hook-straight right (all high)

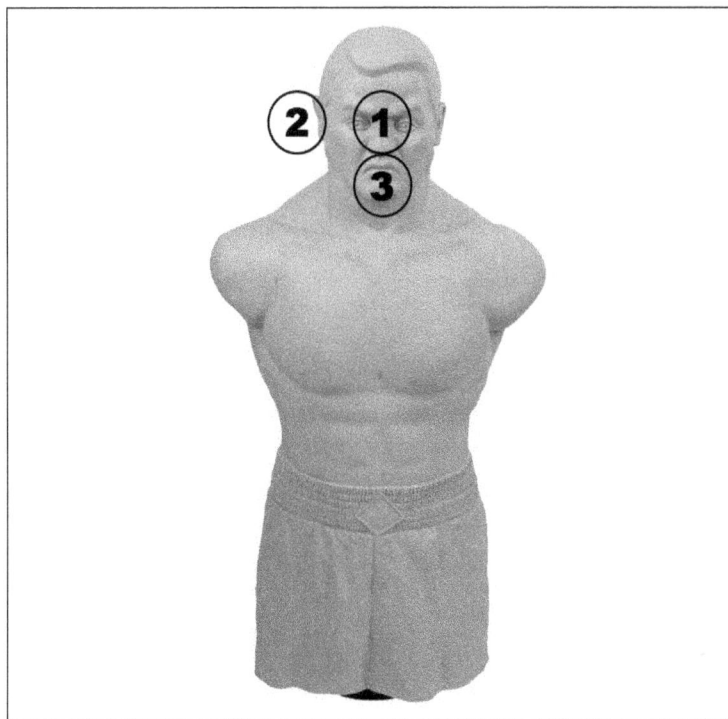

To perform the combination:

1. Jab high at the bag.

2. From the same arm, deliver a high lead hook.

3. Next, throw a straight right.

4. Return to the fighting stance.

Combination #28: jab-lead hook-straight right (low-low-high)

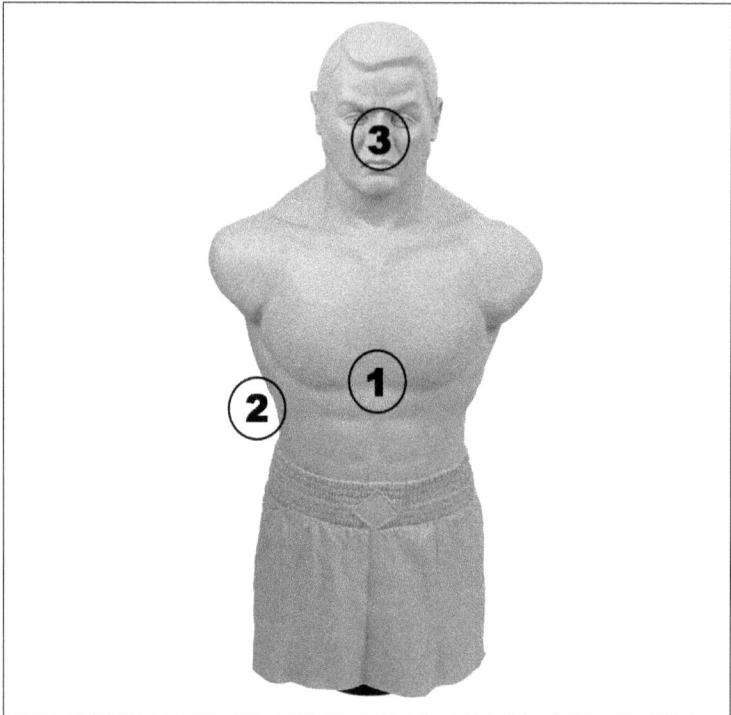

To perform the combination:

1. Jab low at the bag.

2. Next, deliver a low lead hook to the ribs.

3. Follow up with a straight right to the head.

4. Return to the fighting stance.

Combination #29: jab-lead hook-rear hook (all high)

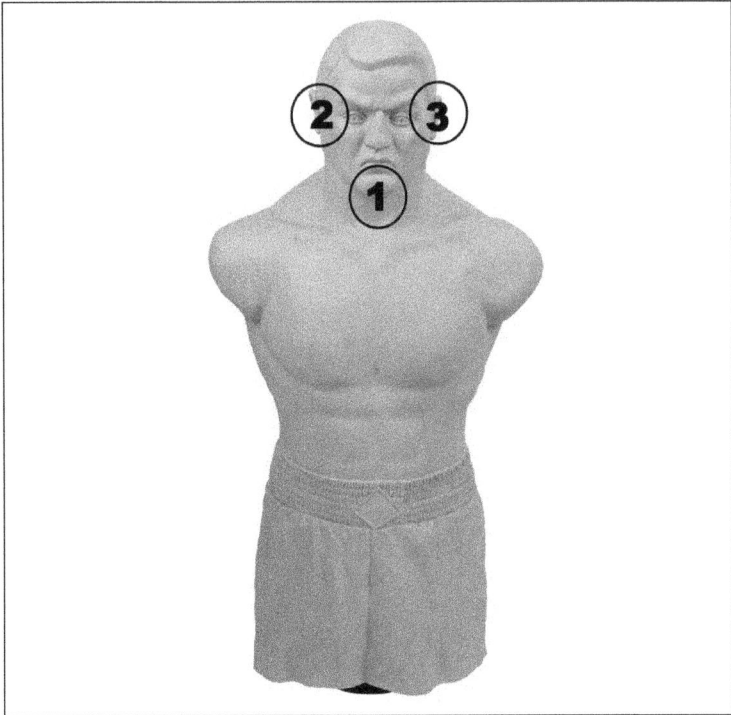

To perform the combination:

1. Jab high at the bag.

2. Next, from the same arm, deliver a high lead hook.

3. Follow up with a high rear hook.

4. Return to the fighting stance.

Combination #30: jab-lead hook-straight right-lead hook (all high)

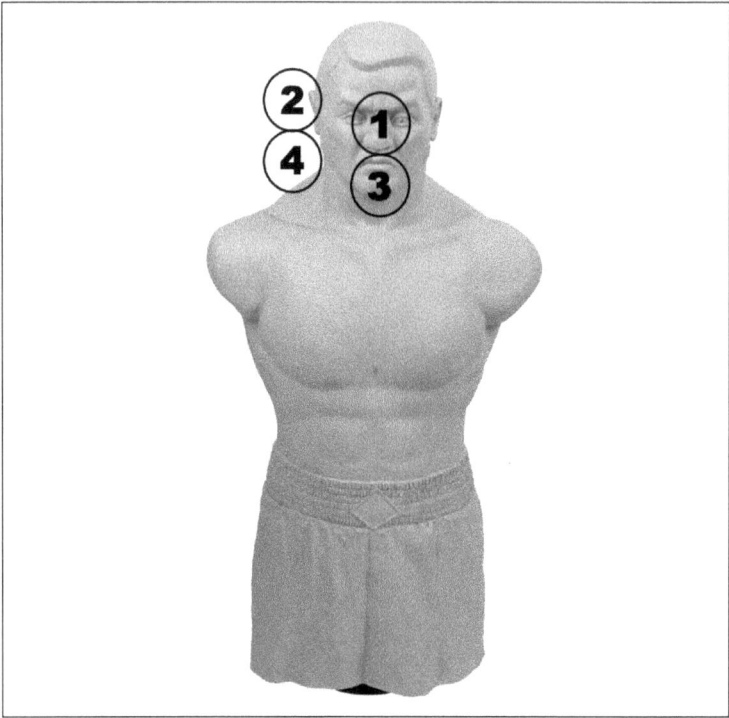

To perform the combination:

1. Jab high at the bag.

2. Next, from the same arm, deliver a high lead hook.

3. Follow up with a straight right.

4. Finish with a high lead hook.

5. Return to the fighting stance.

Combination #31: jab-lead hook-rear hook (high-low-low)

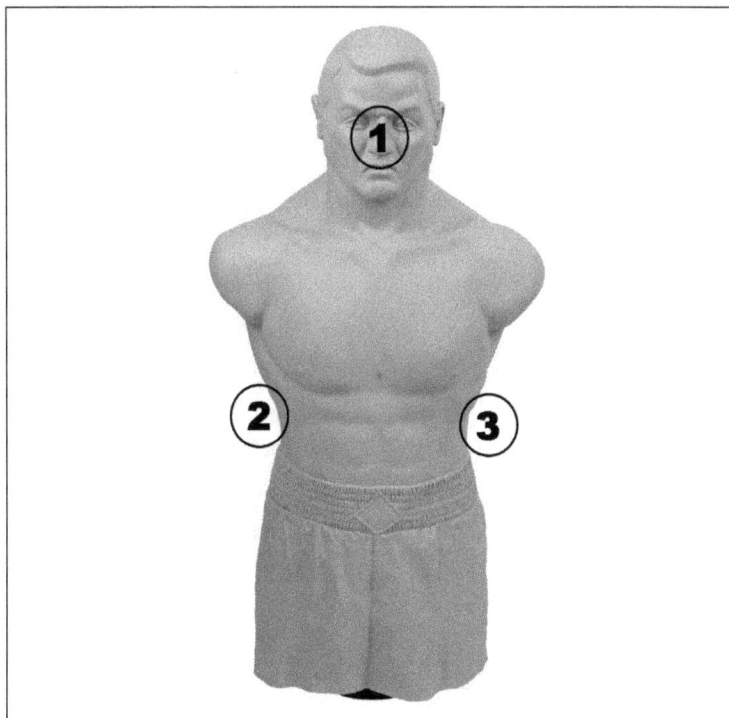

To perform the combination:

1. Jab high at the bag.

2. Next, deliver a low lead hook to the ribs.

3. Follow up with a low rear hook to the ribs.

4. Return to the fighting stance.

Combination #32: jab-lead hook-rear hook (high-high-low)

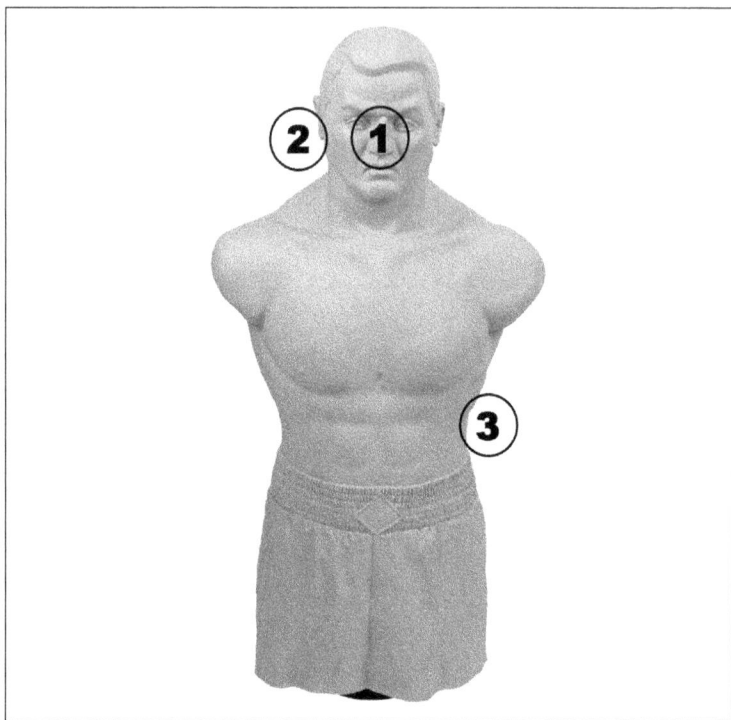

To perform the combination:

1. Jab high at the bag.

2. Next, from the same arm, deliver a high lead hook.

3. Follow up with a low rear hook to the ribs.

4. Return to the fighting stance.

Combination #33: jab-lead hook-rear hook (high-low-high)

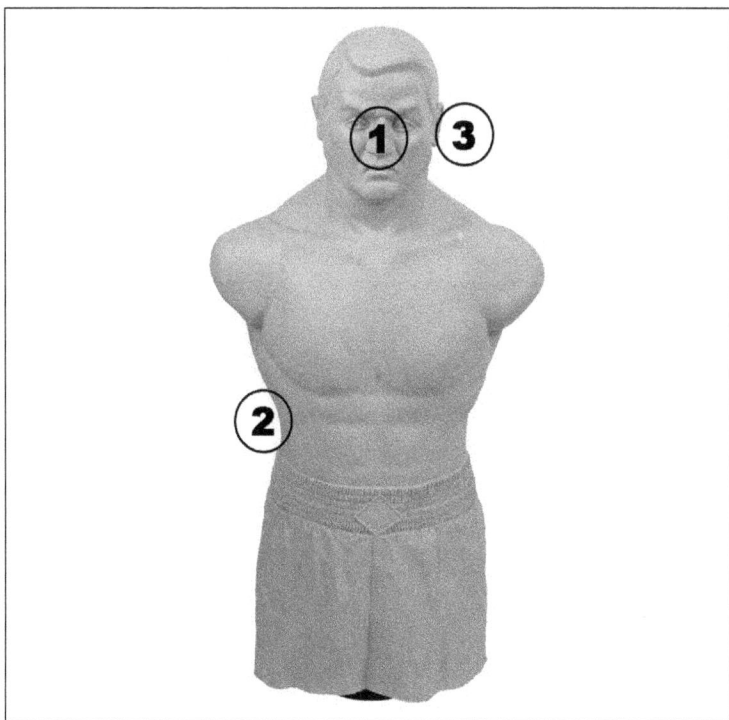

To perform the combination:

1. Jab high at the bag.

2. Next, from the same arm, deliver a lead hook to the ribs.

3. Follow up with a high rear hook to the head.

4. Return to the fighting stance.

Combination #34: jab-jab-straight right-lead hook (all high)

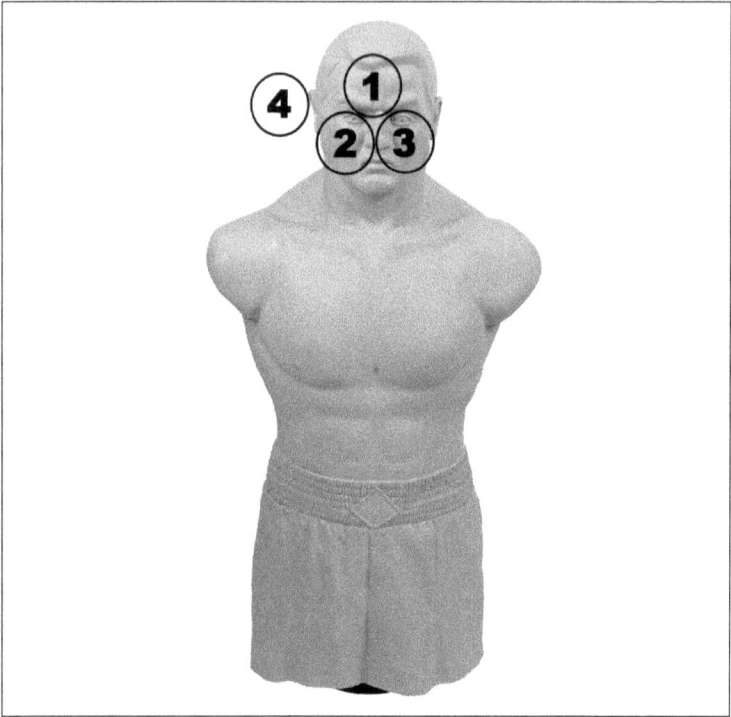

To perform the combination:

1. Jab high at the bag.

2. Follow up with another high jab.

3. Next, throw a high straight right.

4. A high lead hook completes the compound attack.

5. Return to the fighting stance.

Combination #35: jab-jab-straight right-lead hook (high-high-high-low)

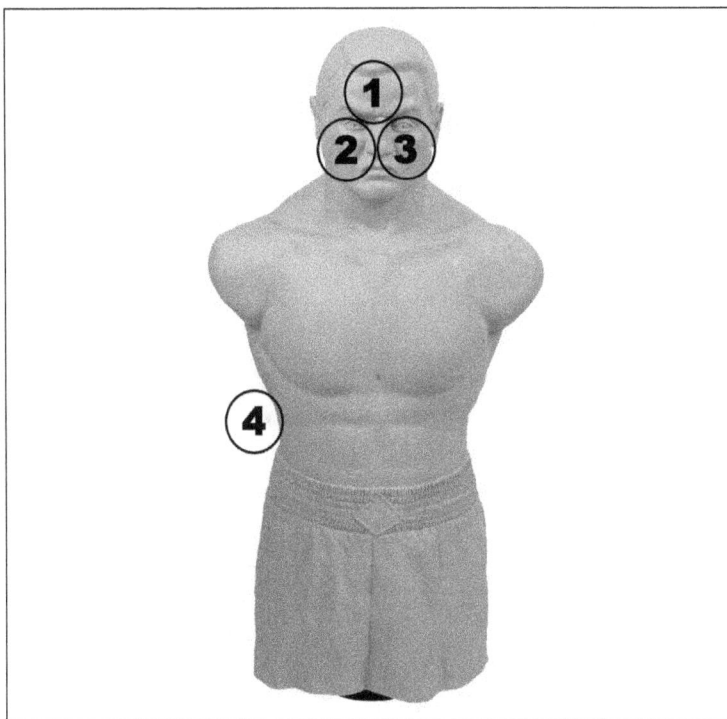

To perform the combination:

1. Jab high at the bag.

2. Follow up with another high jab.

3. Next, throw a high straight right.

4. Finish with a low lead hook to the ribs.

5. Return to the fighting stance.

Combination #36: straight right-lead hook-lead hook-rear hook (low-high-high-low)

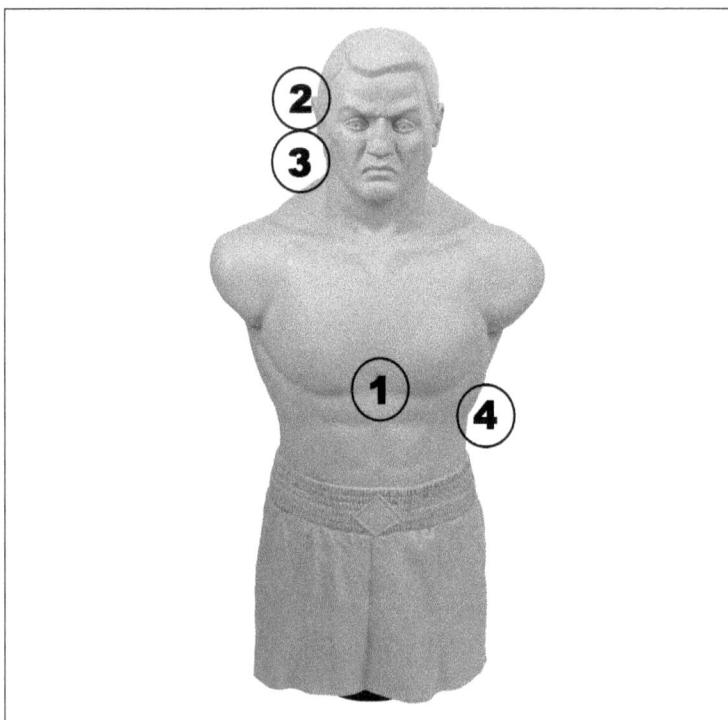

To perform the combination:

1. Deliver a low straight right at the bag.

2. Next, a high lead hook.

3. Throw another high lead hook at the bag.

4. Finish with a low rear hook to the ribs.

5. Return to the fighting stance.

Combination #37: straight right-lead hook-lead hook-rear hook (high-low-low-high)

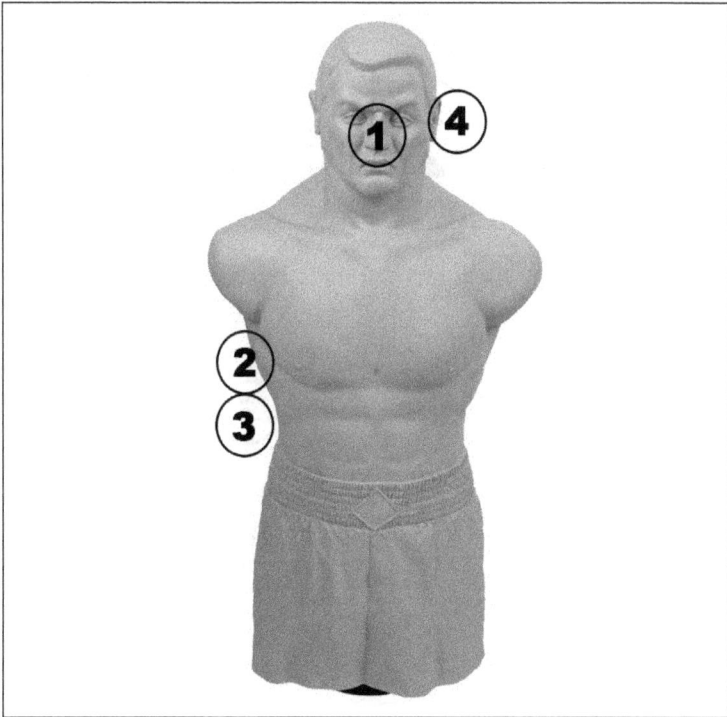

To perform the combination:

1. Throw a high straight right.

2. Next, a low lead hook to the ribs.

3. Deliver another low lead hook to the bag.

4. Finish with a high rear hook.

5. Return to the fighting stance.

Combination 38: straight right-lead hook-straight right-lead hook-rear hook (high-high-low-high-low)

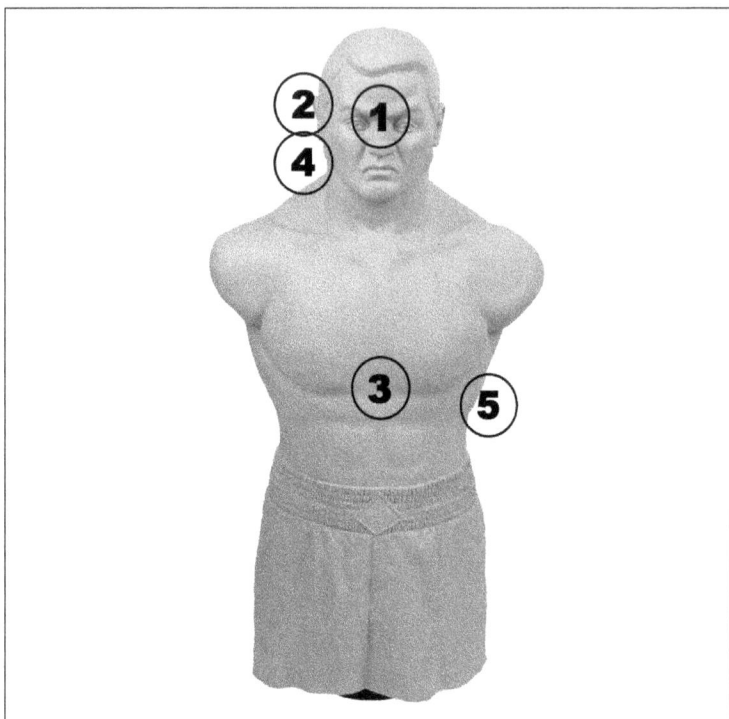

To perform the combination:

1. Throw a high straight right.
2. Next, a high lead hook at the bag.
3. Follow with a low straight right.
4. Deliver another high lead hook.
5. Finish with a low rear hook to the ribs.
6. Return to the fighting stance.

Combination 39: straight right-rear hook-rear hook-lead hook-lead hook (high-high-low-low-low-high)

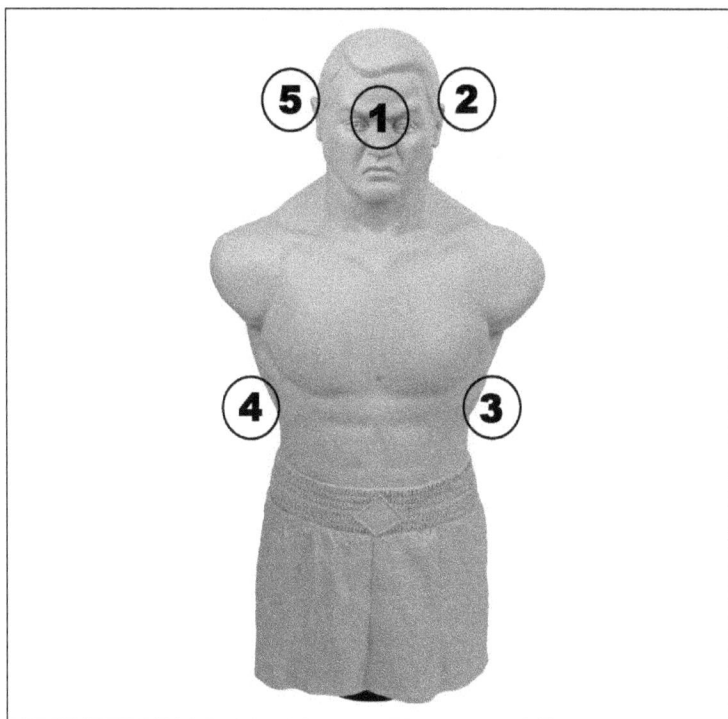

To perform the combination:

1. Throw a high straight right.

2. Next, a high rear hook.

3. Deliver a low rear hook.

4. Follow with a low lead hook to the ribs.

5. Finish with a high lead hook.

6. Return to the fighting stance.

Body Opponent Bag Combinations

Chapter 6
Advanced Combinations

Body Opponent Bag Combinations

Adding Uppercuts to Your Combinations

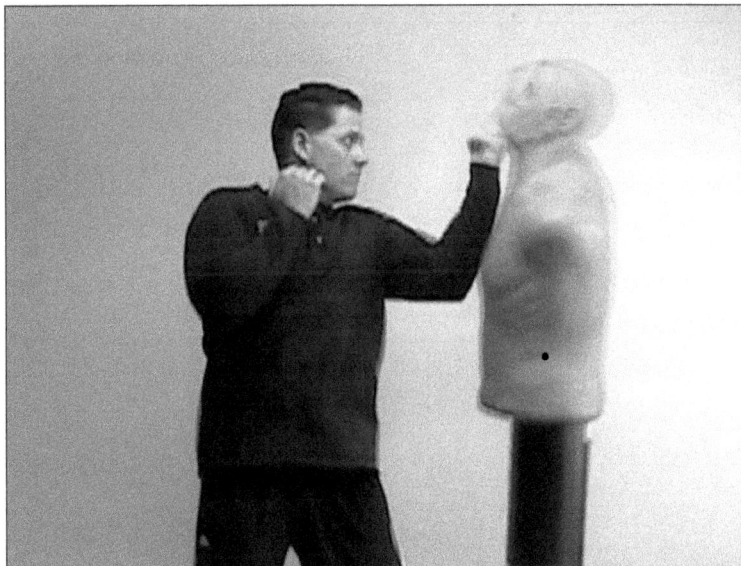

In this chapter, we are going to build off the combinations from the previous two chapters and add uppercuts to your Body Opponent Bag combinations.

The uppercut is an explosive and powerful close-quarter punch that travels in a vertical trajectory to its target. Uppercuts can also be delivered from either your lead or rear arm.

To execute the uppercut, quickly twist and lift your body in the direction of the blow. Make sure that the punch has a short arc and that you avoid any "winding up" motion. A properly executed uppercut should feel like an explosive jolt.

Once again, if you require more information about performing the uppercut, please see Chapter 3 of this book.

Combination #40: jab-jab-rear uppercut (all high)

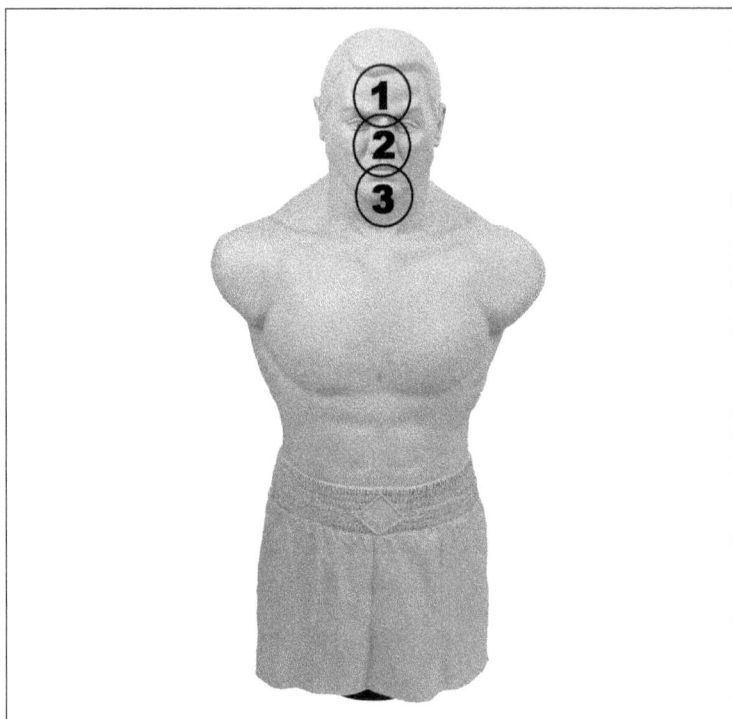

To perform the combination:

1. Jab high at the bag.

2. Quickly retract your punch and throw another jab.

3. Next, throw a rear uppercut to the chin.

4. Return to the fighting stance.

Combination #41: jab-lead uppercut-straight right (all high)

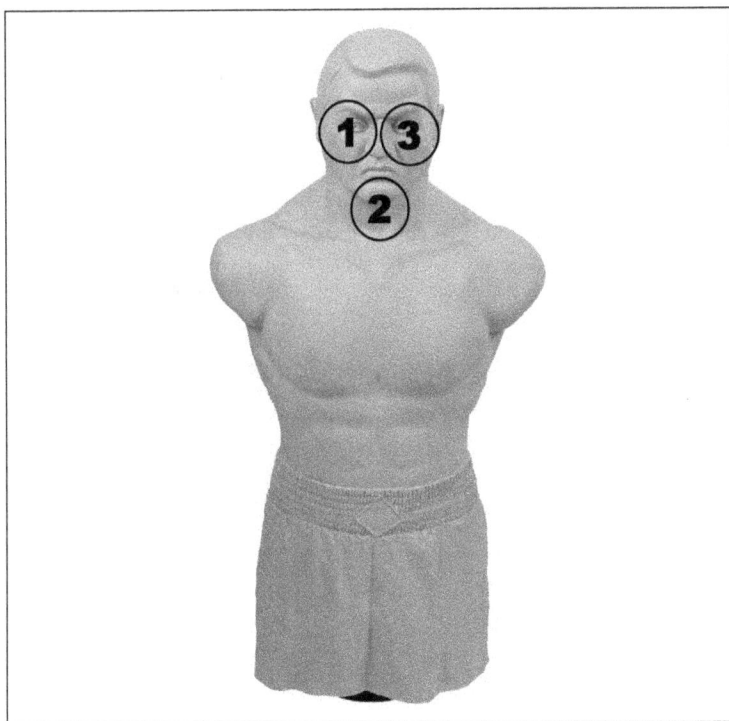

To perform the combination:

1. Jab high at the bag.

2. Quickly retract your punch and throw a lead uppercut.

3. Next, throw a straight right.

4. Return to the fighting stance.

Combination #42: jab-lead uppercut-straight right (low-high-low)

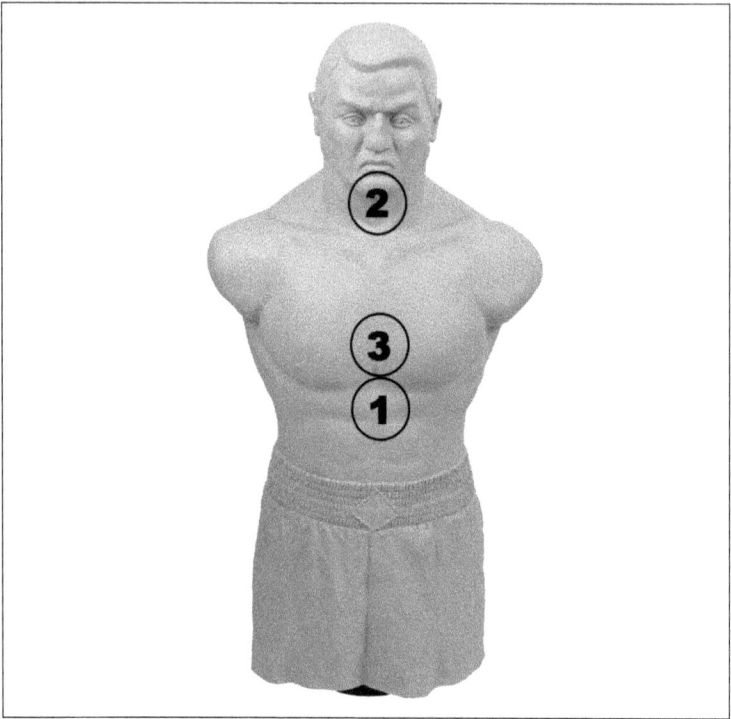

To perform the combination:

1. Jab low at the bag.

2. Next, throw a lead uppercut to the chin.

3. Finish with a low straight right.

4. Return to the fighting stance.

Combination #43: jab-rear uppercut-lead uppercut (all high)

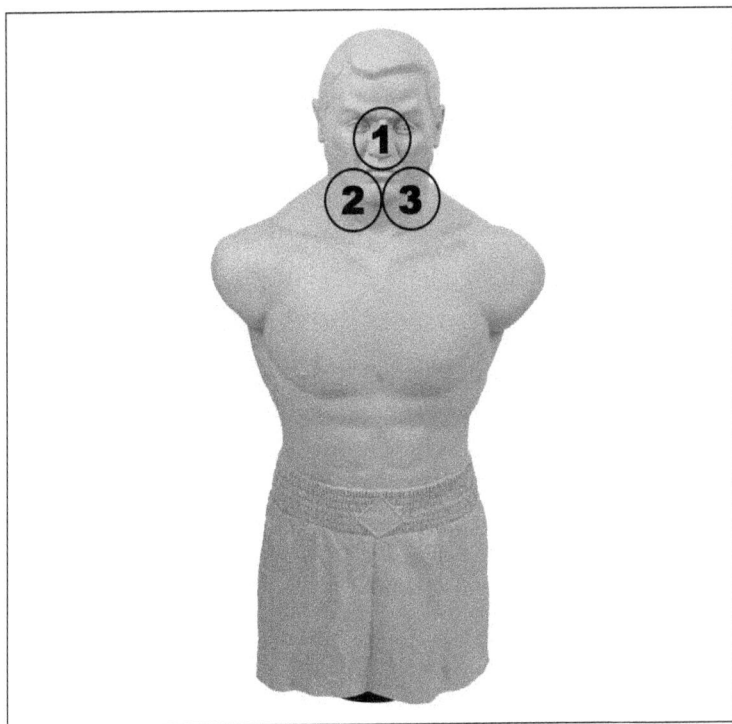

To perform the combination:

1. Jab high at the bag.

2. Next, throw a rear uppercut to the chin.

3. Finish with a lead uppercut to the chin.

4. Return to the fighting stance.

Combination #44: jab-rear uppercut-lead uppercut-straight right-lead hook (all high)

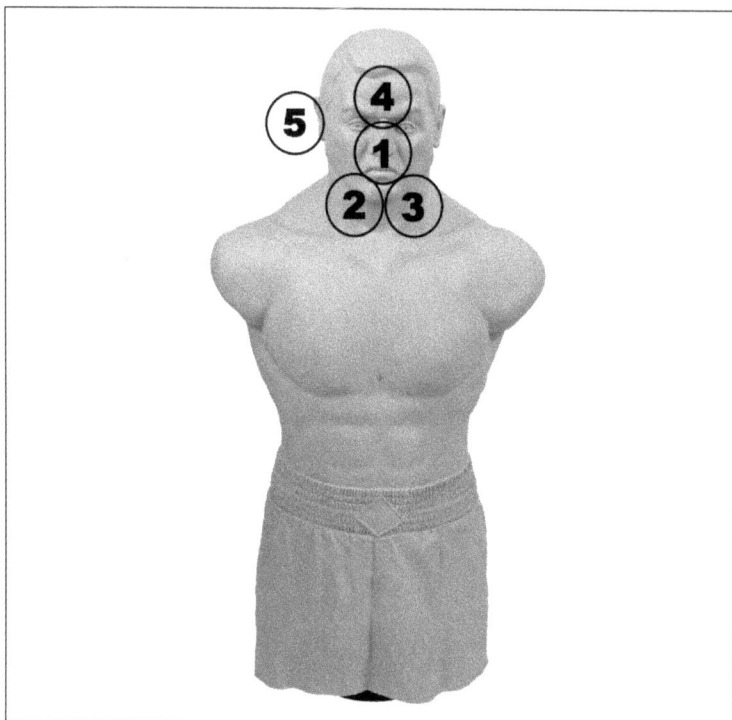

To perform the combination:

1. Jab high at the bag.

2. Next, throw a rear uppercut to the chin.

3. Follow with a lead uppercut to the chin.

4. Throw a high straight right.

5. Finish with a high lead hook.

6. Return to the fighting stance.

Combination #45: jab-straight right-lead hook-rear uppercut (all high)

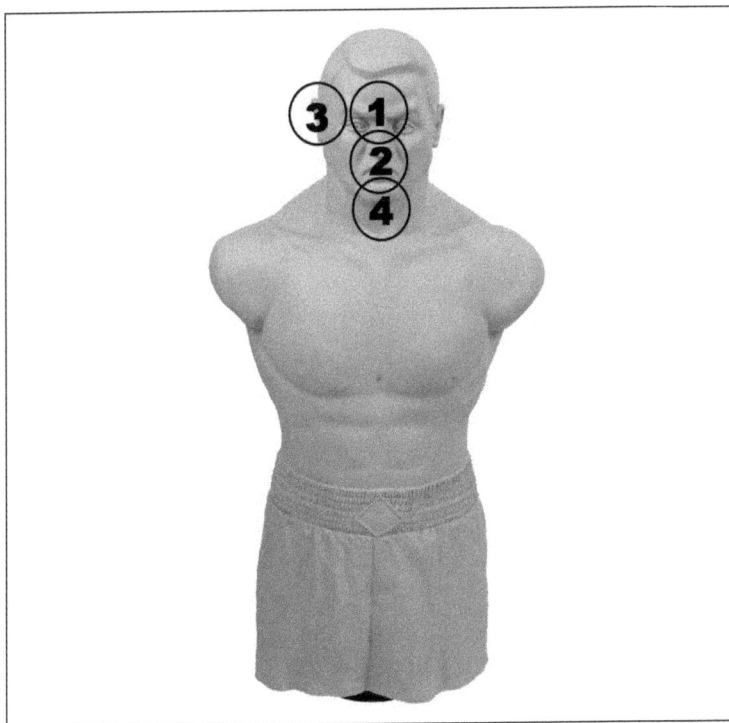

To perform the combination:

1. Jab high at the bag.

2. Next, throw a high straight right.

3. Follow with a high lead hook.

4. Finish with a rear uppercut to the chin.

5. Return to the fighting stance.

Combination #46: jab-rear uppercut-lead hook-straight right (all high)

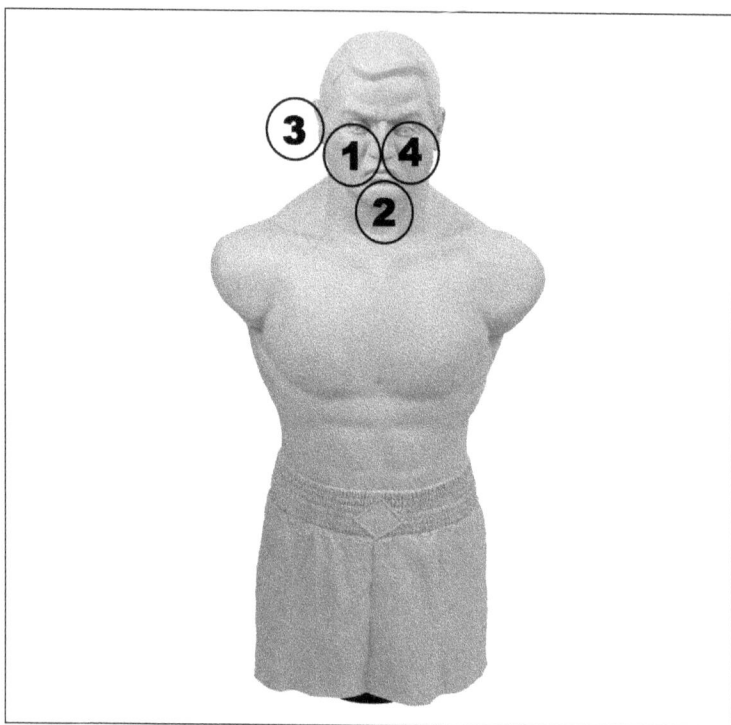

To perform the combination:

1. Jab high at the bag.
2. Next, throw a rear uppercut to the chin.
3. Follow with a lead hook to the head.
4. Throw a high straight right.
5. Return to the fighting stance.

Combination #47: jab-straight right-lead hook-straight right-lead hook-lead hook (5x high-1 low)

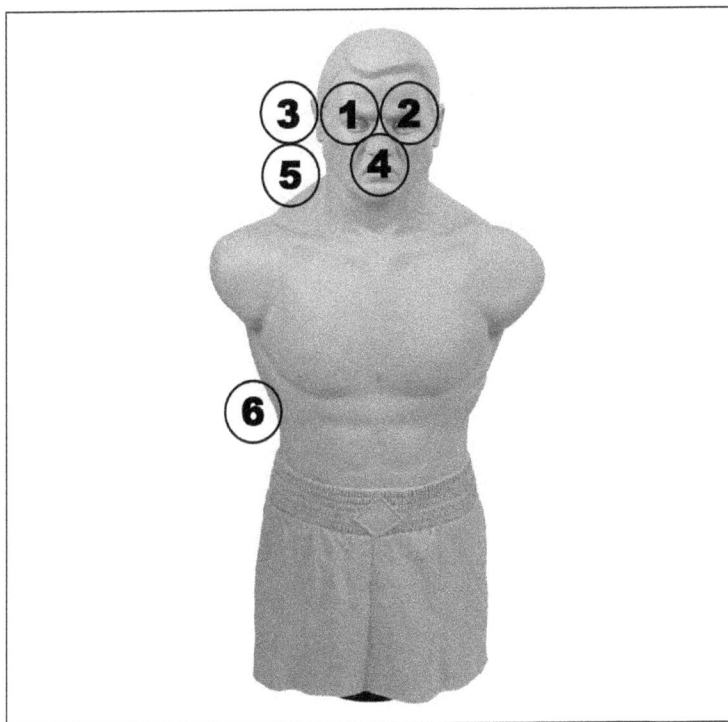

To perform the combination:

1. Jab high at the bag.

2. Next, throw a high straight right.

3. Follow with a lead hook to the head.

4. Throw a high straight right.

5. Next, a lead hook to the head.

6. Finish with a low lead hook to the ribs

7. Return to the fighting stance.

Combination #48: straight right-lead uppercut-rear hook (all high)

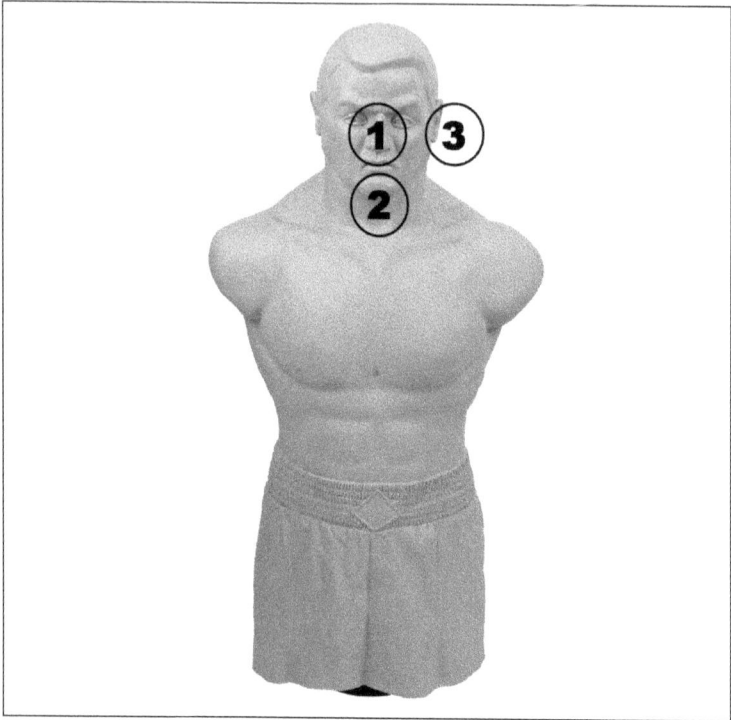

To perform the combination:

1. Start with a high straight right.

2. Next, throw a lead uppercut to the chin.

3. Follow with a rear hook to the head.

4. Return to the fighting stance.

Combination #49: straight right-jab-rear hook-lead uppercut-rear hook (high-high-low-high-high)

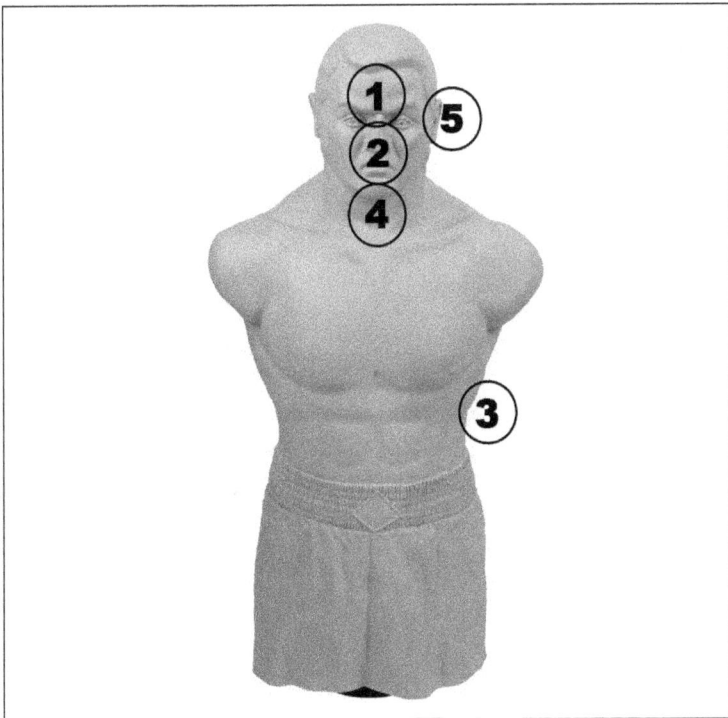

To perform the combination:

1. Start with a high straight right.

2. Next, throw a high jab.

3. Follow with a low rear hook to the ribs.

4. Throw a lead uppercut to the chin.

5. Finish with a high rear hook.

6. Return to the fighting stance.

Combination #50: straight right-lead hook-straight right-lead hook-rear uppercut (high-high-high-low-high)

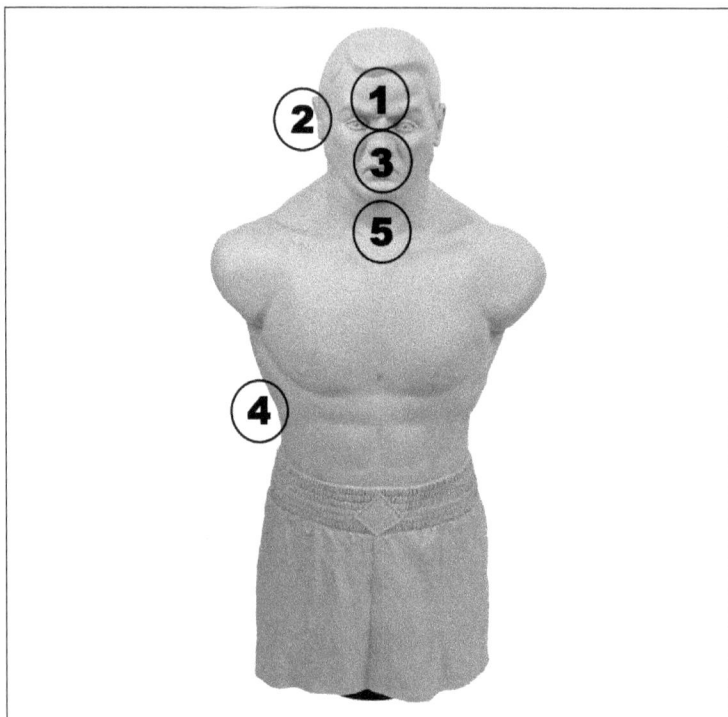

To perform the combination:

1. Start with a high straight right.

2. Next, throw a high lead hook.

3. Follow with another high straight right.

4. Throw a lead hook to the ribs.

5. Finish with a rear uppercut to the chin.

6. Return to the fighting stance.

Combination #51: rear hook-lead hook-rear hook-lead uppercut (all high)

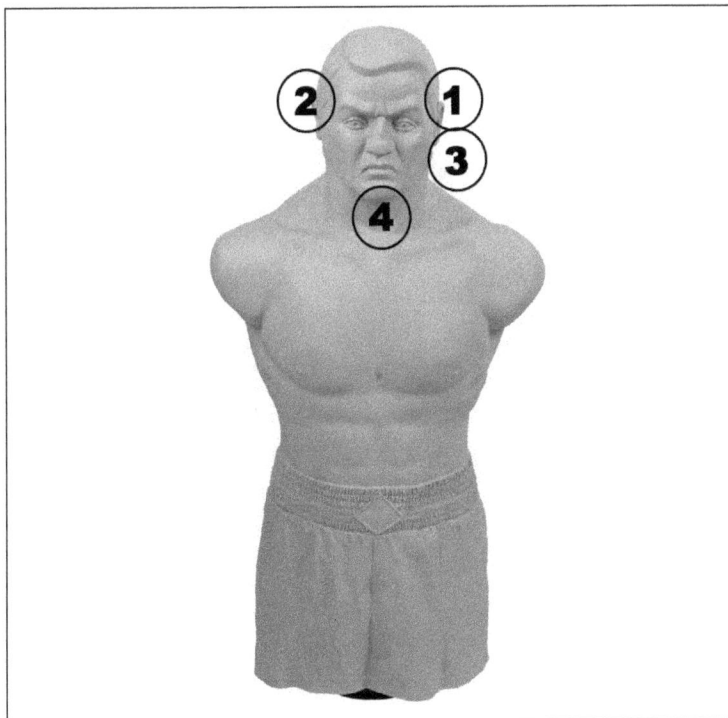

To perform the combination:

1. Start with a high rear hook.

2. Next, throw a high lead hook.

3. Follow with another high rear hook.

4. Finish with a lead uppercut.

5. Return to the fighting stance.

Combination #52: rear hook-lead hook-rear hook-lead hook-rear uppercut (high-low-low-low-high)

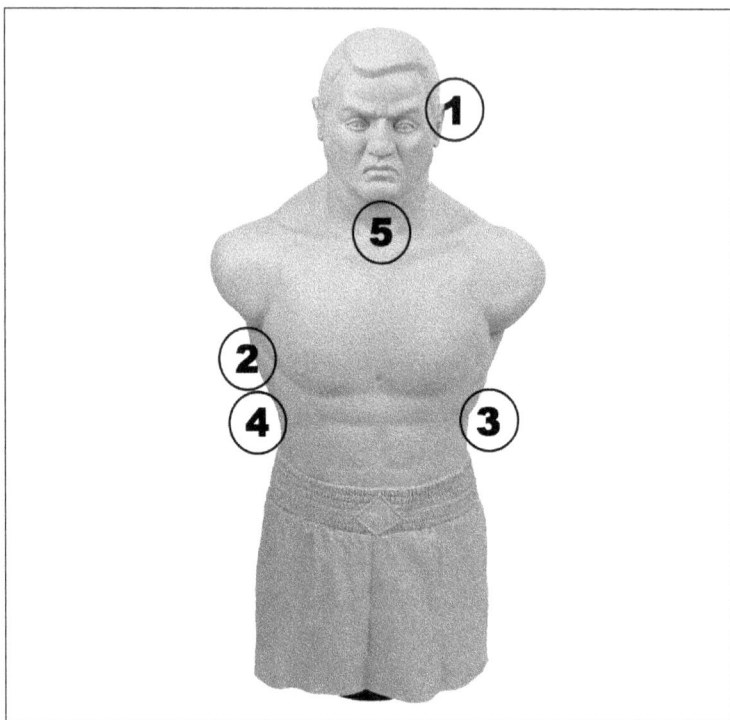

To perform the combination:

1. Start with a high rear hook.

2. Next, throw a lead hook to the ribs.

3. Follow with rear hook to the ribs.

4. Throw another lead hook to the ribs.

5. Finish with a rear uppercut to the chin.

6. Return to the fighting stance.

Combination #53: rear uppercut-lead uppercut-rear hook-lead hook (all high)

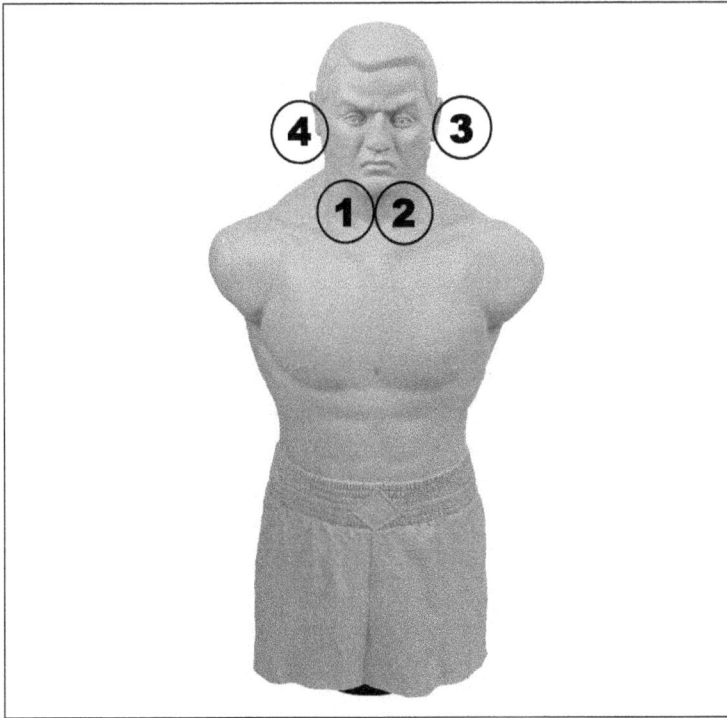

To perform the combination:

1. Start with a rear uppercut to the chin.

2. Next, throw a lead uppercut to the chin.

3. Follow with rear hook to the head.

4. Finish with a lead hook to the head

5. Return to the fighting stance.

Combination #54: rear uppercut-lead uppercut-rear uppercut-lead uppercut (high-high-low-low)

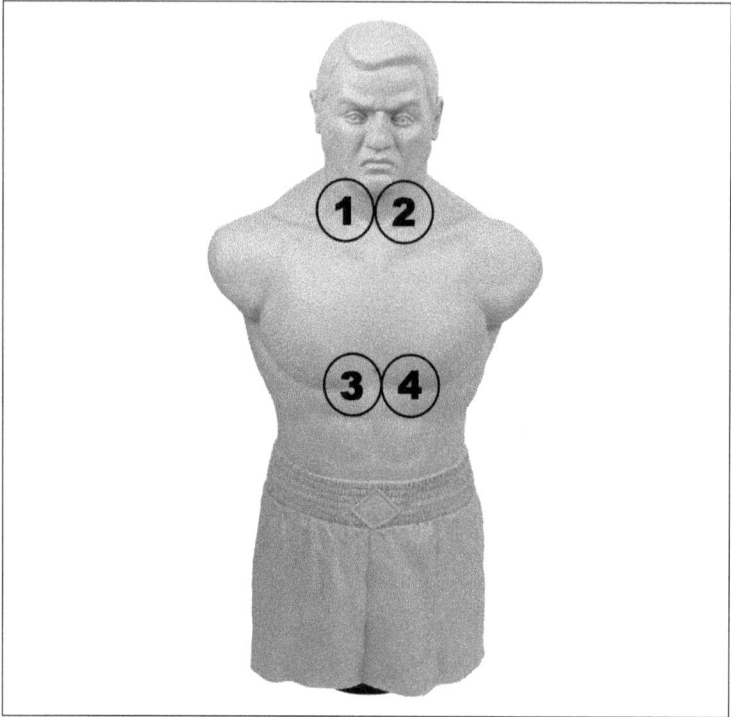

To perform the combination:

1. Start with a rear uppercut to the chin.

2. Next, throw a lead uppercut to the chin.

3. Follow with rear uppercut to the solar plexus.

4. Finish with a lead uppercut to the solar plexus.

5. Return to the fighting stance.

Combination #55: lead uppercut-rear uppercut-lead uppercut-rear hook-lead hook-rear hook (all high)

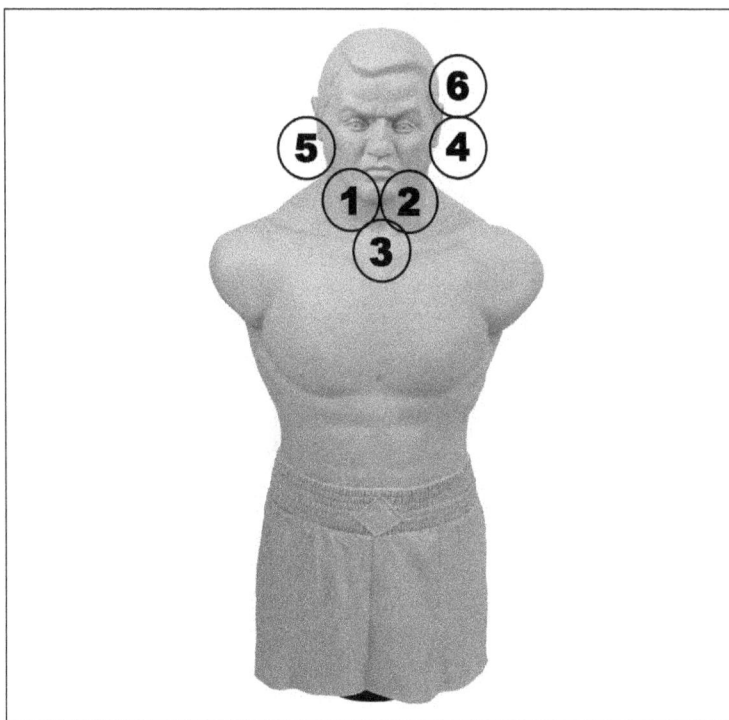

To perform the combination:

1. Start with a lead uppercut to the chin.

2. Next, throw a rear uppercut to the chin.

3. Follow with another lead uppercut.

4. Throw a high rear hook.

5. Next, a high lead hook.

6. Finish with another high rear hook.

7. Return to the fighting stance.

Combination #56: rear uppercut-lead hook-rear hook-lead uppercut-lead hook (high-high-high-low-low)

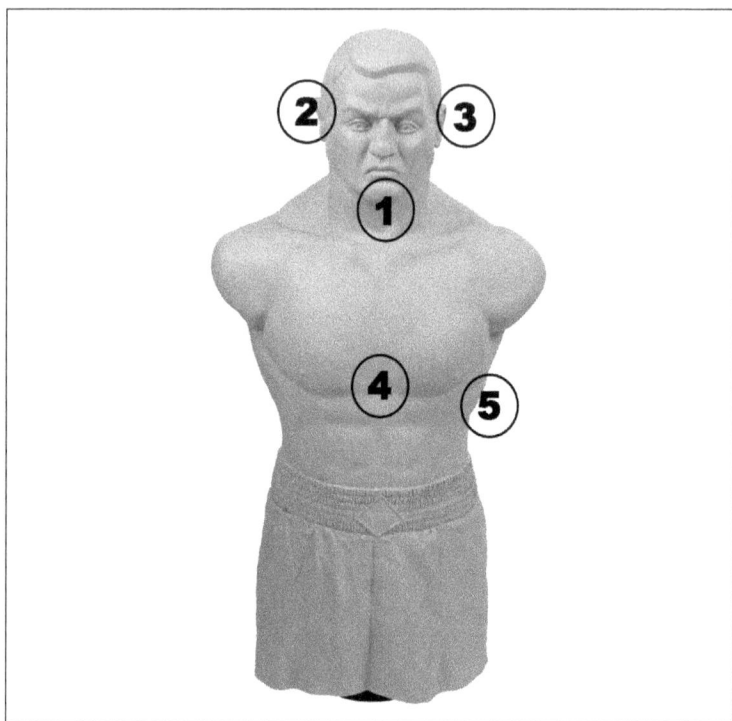

To perform the combination:

1. Start with a lead uppercut to the chin.

2. Next, throw a high lead hook.

3. Follow with a high rear hook.

4. Throw a low lead uppercut to the solar plexus.

5. Finish with a low rear hook to the ribs.

6. Return to the fighting stance.

Combination #57: jab-straight right-lead & rear hook-lead & rear uppercuts (all high)

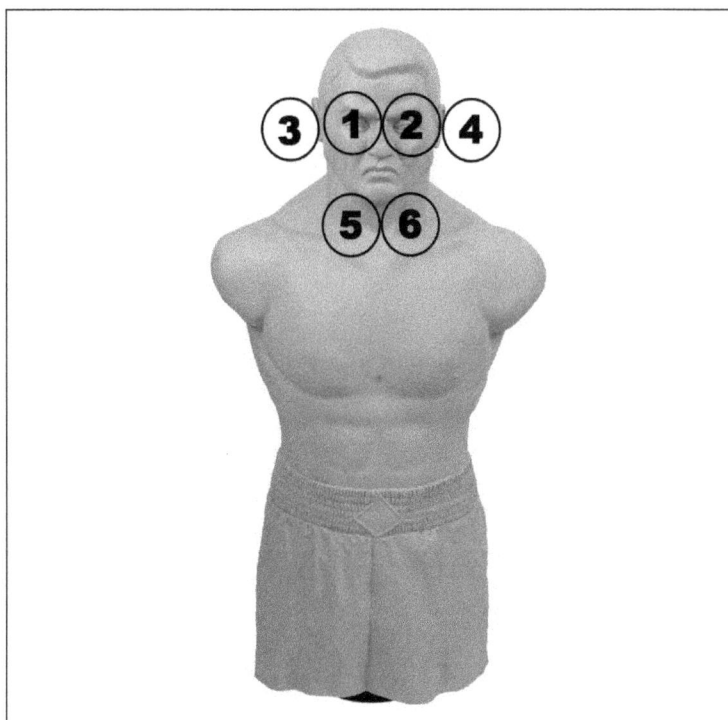

To perform the combination:

1. Start with a high jab.

2. Next, throw a high straight right.

3. Follow with a high lead hook.

4. Throw a high rear hook.

5. Throw a lead uppercut to the chin.

6. Finish with a rear uppercut to the chin.

7. Return to the fighting stance.

Body Opponent Bag Combinations

Chapter 7
Body Opponent Bag Workouts

Body Opponent Bag Combinations

Time-Based Body Opponent Bag Training

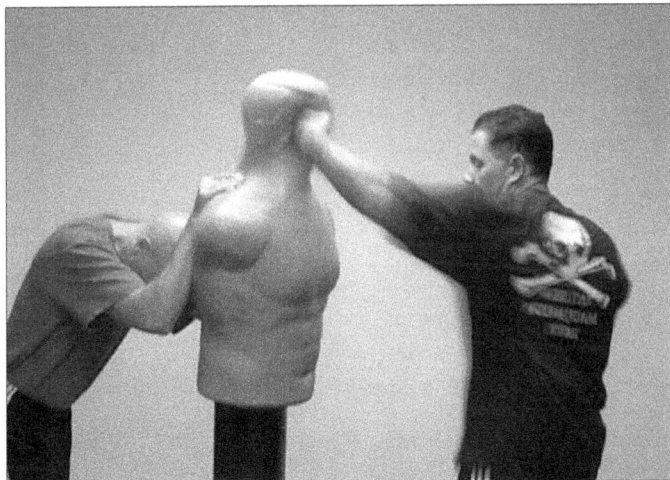

In many of my previous books, I discussed the importance of creating time-based workouts. Essentially, a time-based workout is predicated on "rounds" and it's the best way to organize your Body Opponent Bag workout. Before you begin, however, you need to decide on the duration of your rounds as well as the rest intervals.

For example, mixed martial artists, boxers and kick boxers will often hit the bag for three-minute rounds and then rest for a one-minute period. Depending on their level of conditioning and specific training goals, they might do this for a total of five to eight rounds.

Initially, you'll need to experiment with both the round duration and rest intervals to see what works best for you. Remember to start off slow and progressively build up the intensity and duration of your workouts.

To get you started on the right track, I have included some sample time-based workouts you might want to try. Keep in mind, the advanced level workouts are for elite athletes who have a minimum of three years of bag training.

Sample Time Based BOB Workouts

Skill Level	Duration of Each Round	Rest Period	Total Number of rounds
Beginner	1 minute	2 minutes	3
Beginner	1 minute	1 minute	3
Beginner	2 minutes	2 minute	3
Beginner	2 minutes	1 minute	3
Intermediate	3 minutes	2 minutes	5
Intermediate	3 minutes	1 minute	5
Intermediate	3 minutes	2 minute	6
Intermediate	3 minutes	1 minute	6
Advanced	4 minutes	2 minutes	8
Advanced	4 minutes	1 minute	8
Advanced	5 minutes	2 minutes	10
Advanced	5 minutes	1 minute	10

A Word of Caution Before you Start Training!

Take your time when working out on the bag. If you are learning how to use the Body Opponent Bag for the very first time, I strongly urge you to take your time and develop the proper punching body mechanics before tearing into the bag.

Remember, the Body Opponent Bag is a serious piece of training equipment and it's easy to get injured when using it. Body Opponent Bag workouts are also tough and very demanding on the body. Avoid premature exhaustion by pacing yourself during your workouts. Remember, it's not a race! Enjoy the process of learning how to use the bag with skill and finesse.

Warning! Before you begin any exercise program, including those suggested in this book, it is important to check with your physician to see if you have any condition that might be aggravated by strenuous exercise.

BOB Combination Blending

All of the punching combinations featured in this book are both foundational and challenging and will keep you busy for many years to come. In fact, you can make significant progress by sticking with the basic combinations featured in each chapter and just performing them over and over again for the duration of your round.

However, for those of you who require a greater challenge in your Body Opponent Bag training, you can perform "*combination blending.*" Essentially, combination blending is strategically combining two Body Opponent Bag combinations into one seamless combination duration a training round.

For example, if you are a beginner, you would pick two combination sequences from *Chapter 4: (Beginner Combinations)* of this book. For instance, you might pick combination #1 and combination #17.

- **Combination #1: jab-jab (high-high)**
- **Combination #17: jab-straight right-jab-straight right (all low)**

Next, you would combine the two punching sequences and perform them on the Body Opponent Bag for the duration of a three minute round. The entire combination sequence would look like the following:

Combination Blending Example: Combination 1+17= jab-jab (high-high) jab-straight right-jab-straight right (all low)

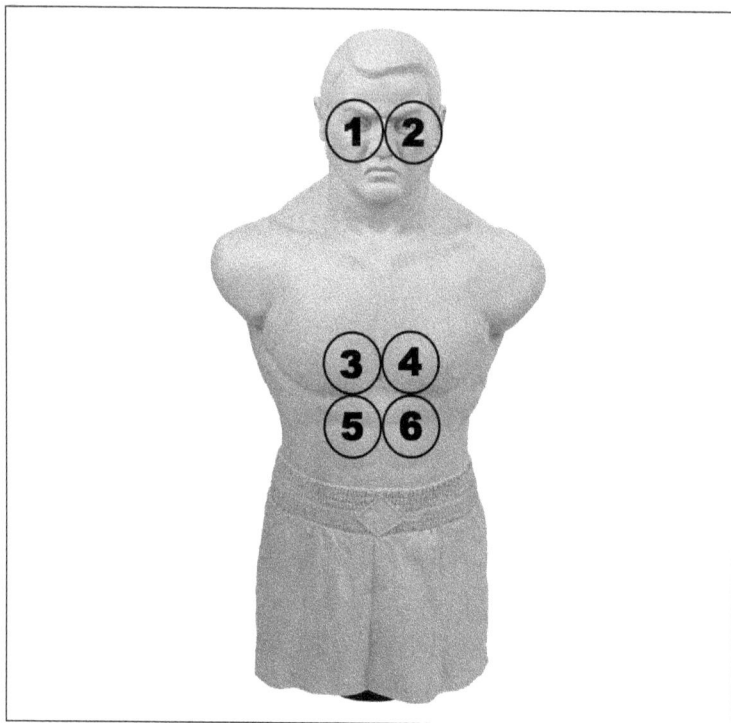

To perform the combination:

1. Jab high at the bag.
2. Throw a high straight right.
3. Jab low at the bag.
4. Next, throw a low straight right.
5. Follow up with another low jab.
6. Finish with a low straight right.
7. Return to the stance position.

Here's another example of combination blending. However, this time we are going to blend combinations for an advanced practitioner. This requires you to pick *at least one* combination sequence from *Chapter 6: (Advanced Combinations)* and add it to any another sequences featured in this book. For instance, you might pick combination #42 from the Advanced Combinations and Beginner Combination #7.

- **Combination #42: jab-lead uppercut-straight right (low-high-low)**

- **Combination #7: straight right-jab (all high)**

Next, you would combine the two sequences and perform them on the Body Opponent Bag for the duration of your round. This sequence would look like the following:

- **Combination 42+7 = jab-lead uppercut-straight right (low-high-low)+straight right-jab (all high)**

Combination 42+7 = jab-lead uppercut-straight right (low-high-low)+straight right-jab (all high)

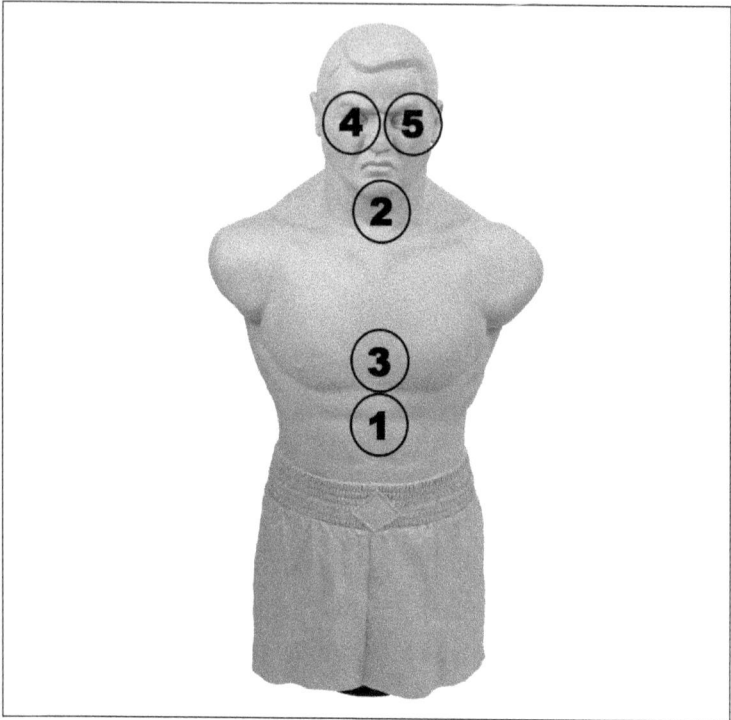

To perform the combination:

1. Jab low at the bag.

2. Next, throw a lead uppercut to the chin.

3. Finish with a low straight right.

4. Return to the fighting stance.

	Blending Combinations		
	Beginner level	Intermediate level	Advanced level
Sequence	1 +2	20+23	40+1
Sequence	1 + 3	25+27	42+25
Sequence	4 + 8	1+28	45+8
Sequence	4 + 12	11+31	5+50
Sequence	5 + 3	12+36	51+19
Sequence	6 + 9	19+34	54+6
Sequence	7 + 13	27+39	10+55
Sequence	8 + 5	33+20	48+12
Sequence	9 + 13	21+22	57+3
Sequence	10 + 14	35+17	47+29
Sequence	11 + 8	24+30	44+13
Sequence	14 + 1	26+2	49+58

Is Combination Blending Necessary?

Some of you might be wondering if combination blending is necessary for Body Opponent Bag training? Or if some of the combination sequences are too lengthy for practical punching applications. After all, how many punches does one really need for an effective compound attack? Well, the answer to these questions really depends on the individual and their personal training goals. Nevertheless, I've included combination blending in this book for

Body Opponent Bag Combinations

some of the following important reasons:

1. It generates a truly unlimited supply of Body Opponent Bag combinations that will literally challenge you for a lifetime.

2. It prevents your workout routines from becoming boring, stagnant, and monotonous.

3. It's a great mental toughness exercise that develops important attributes like attention control, instrumental aggression, immediate resilience, and self-confidence.

Reversing the Combination Blending Sequence

Combination blending is the most challenging form of Body Opponent Bag training. Like I stated earlier, when used correctly, you can create an infinite amount of punching combinations that will challenge you for the rest of your life!

Moreover, you can also reverse the sequence of the blended combination. For instance, the kinesthetic feel and strategic application of punching sequence 42+48 will be substantially different from 48+42. If you don't believe me, try it out on the Body Opponent Bag and see for yourself.

Create Your Own Punching Combinations

To get you into the creative process of developing punching combinations, I have provided a section for you to write down your own Body Opponent Bag combinations.

1.

2.

3.

4.

5.

6.

7.

8.

9.

10.

11.

12.

13.

14.

15.

16.

17.

18.

Body Opponent Bag Combinations

19.

20.

21.

22.

23.

24.

25.

26.

27.

28.

29.

30.

31.

32.

33.

34.

35.

36.

37.

38.

39.

40.

You Need to Move Around the BOB

To ensure that you would clearly understand all of the principles featured in this book, I intentionally had every punching technique demonstrated from a stationary position.

However, when working out on the Body Opponent Bag, you should always move around. This concept is important for some of the following important reasons:

1. It increases the overall intensity of your Body Opponent Bag workout.

2. It amplifies the power of your punches.

3. It gives you a greater understanding and appreciation of fighting ranges.

4. It develops good fighting habits. For example, it makes you a more elusive target when fighting an actual opponent.

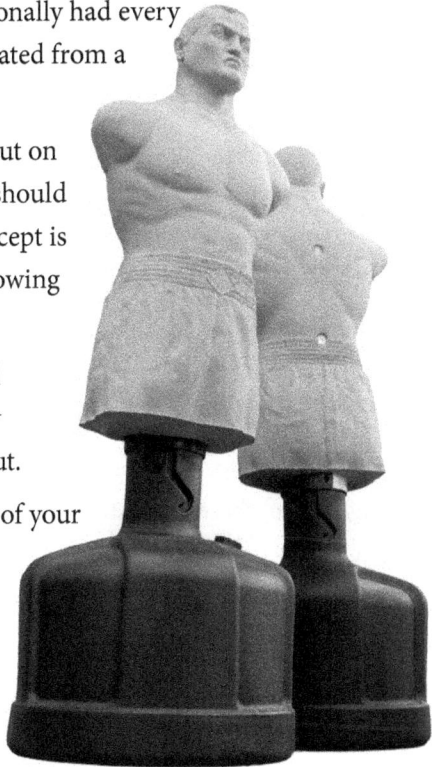

Combination Blending Tips

It's important not to exceed your skill level when performing combination blending. For example, if you're a beginner, never integrate advanced or intermediate combinations into your Body Opponent Bag workout. Be patient and stick to guidelines outlined in this book.

However, intermediate practitioners are encouraged to integrate beginner level combinations with combination blending. Likewise, advanced practitioners may add beginner and intermediate punching combinations with advanced combinations. Please refer to the accompanying chart for more information.

For your convenience, I have also provided several combination blending samples for beginner, intermediate, and advanced levels of training. Again, these are just examples of what you can do in your training.

Punching Combination Review

For your convenience, I have provided a list of all of the punching combinations featured in each of the previous chapters.

Chapter 4: Beginner Combinations

1. jab-jab (all high)

2. jab-jab (all low)

3. jab-jab (high-low)

4. jab-jab (low-high)

5. jab-straight right (all high)

6. jab-straight right (high-low)

7. straight right-jab (all high)

8. jab-straight right-straight right (all high)

9. straight right-jab-straight right-jab (all high)

10. jab-jab-straight right (all high)

11. jab-jab-straight right (high-high-low)

12. jab-straight right-jab (all high)

13. jab-straight right-jab (high-low-high)

14. jab-straight right-jab-straight right (all high)

15. jab-straight right-jab-straight right (high-low-high-low)

16. jab-straight right-jab-straight right (low-high-low-high)

17. jab-straight right-jab-straight right (all low)

18. jab-jab-straight right (low-low-high)

19. jab-jab-jab (high-low-high)

Chapter 5: Intermediate Combinations

20. jab-straight right-hook (all high)

21. jab-straight right-hook (high-high-low)

22. jab-straight right-hook-hook (all high)

23. jab-straight right-hook-hook (high-high-high-low)

24. jab-straight right-hook-hook (high-high-low-high)

25. jab-rear hook-rear hook (high-high-low)

26. jab-rear hook-rear hook (high-low-high)

27. jab-lead hook-straight right (all high)

28. jab-lead hook-straight right (low-low-high)

29. jab-lead hook-rear hook (all high)

30. jab-lead hook-straight right-lead hook (all high)

31. jab-lead hook-rear hook (high-low-low)

32. jab-lead hook-rear hook (high-high-low)

33. jab-lead hook-rear hook (high-low-high)

34. jab-jab-straight right-lead hook (all high)

35. jab-jab-straight right-lead hook (high-high-high-low)

36. straight right-lead hook-lead hook-rear hook (low-high-high-low)

37. straight right-lead hook-lead hook-rear hook (high-low-low-high)

38. straight right-lead hook-straight right-lead hook-rear hook (high-high-low-high-low)

39. straight right-rear hook-rear hook-lead hook-lead hook (high-high-low-low-low-high)

Chapter 6: Advanced Combinations

40. jab-jab-rear uppercut (all high)

41. jab-lead uppercut-straight right (all high)

42. jab-lead uppercut-straight right (low-high-low)

43. jab-rear uppercut-lead uppercut (all high)

44. jab-rear uppercut-lead uppercut-straight right-lead hook (all high)

45. jab-straight right-lead hook-rear uppercut (all high)

46. jab-rear uppercut-lead hook-straight right (all high)

47. jab-straight right-lead hook-straight right-lead hook-lead hook (5x high-1 low)

48. straight right-lead uppercut-rear hook (all high)

49. straight right-jab-rear hook-lead uppercut-rear hook (high-high-low-high-high)

50. straight right-lead hook-straight right-lead hook-rear uppercut (high-high-high-low-high)

51. rear hook-lead hook-rear hook-lead uppercut (all high)

52. rear hook-lead hook-rear hook-lead hook-rear uppercut (high-low-low-low-high)

53. rear uppercut-lead uppercut-rear hook-lead hook (all high)

54. rear uppercut-lead uppercut-rear uppercut-lead uppercut (high-high-low-low)

55. lead uppercut-rear uppercut-lead uppercut-rear hook-lead hook-rear hook (all high)

56. rear uppercut-lead hook-rear hook-lead uppercut-lead hook (high-high-high-low-low)

57. jab-straight right-lead & rear hook-lead & rear uppercuts (all high)

Adding Kicks, Elbow and Knee Strikes

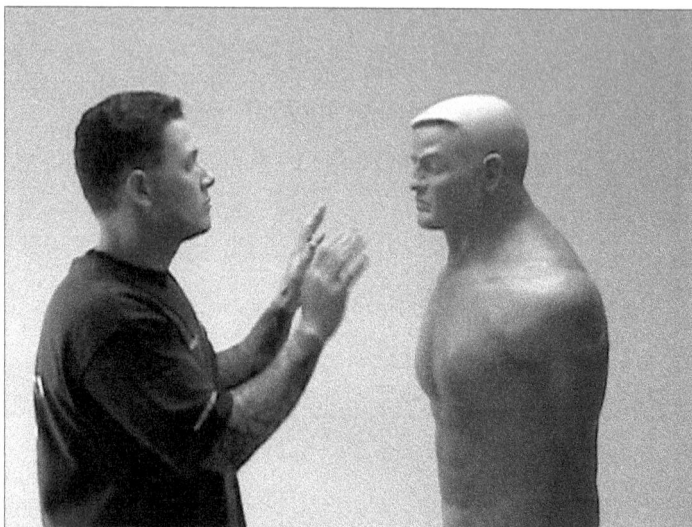

Once you have acquired a modicum of proficiency with the punching combinations featured in this book, you can add kicks, elbow and knee strikes to your training.

For your convenience, I've included a list of fighting combinations that also includes kicks, elbow and knee strikes. Again, these are just sample combinations that you can add to your Body Opponent Bag workout routine.

- Jab - Hook Kick (rear leg)
- Jab - Jab - Hook Kick (rear leg)
- Jab - Straight right - Hook Kick (front leg)
- Jab - Straight Right - Hook Kick (front leg) - Hook Kick (rear)
- Jab - Diagonal Knee (rear)
- Jab - Diagonal Knee (rear) - Diagonal Knee (front)

- Jab - Diagonal Knee (rear) - Horizontal elbow (front)
- Jab - Straight Right - Diagonal Knee (front)
- Jab - Straight Right - Push Kick (rear)
- Jab - Straight Right - Jab - Straight Right - Hook Kick (rear)
- Jab - Straight Right - Jab - Straight Right - Push Kick (rear)
- Jab - Straight Right - Push Kick (rear) - Diagonal Knee (front)
- Jab - Straight Right - Push Kick (rear) - Hook Kick (front)
- Jab - Straight Right - Diagonal Knee (front) - Horizontal Elbow (rear)
- Push Kick (front leg) - Straight Right (high)
- Push Kick (front leg) - Straight Right (low)
- Push Kick (front leg) - Straight Right (high) - Lead Hook (high)
- Push Kick (front leg) - Straight Right (low) - Lead Hook (low)
- Push Kick (front leg) - Straight Right (low) - Lead Hook (high)
- Push Kick (front leg) - Straight Right (high) - Lead Hook (low)
- Push Kick (front leg) - Straight Right (high) - Lead Hook (high) - Rear Hook (high)
- Push Kick (front leg) - Straight Right (high) - Lead Hook (low) - Rear Hook (low)
- Push Kick (front leg) - Rear Uppercut
- Push Kick (front leg) - Rear Uppercut - Lead Uppercut
- Push Kick (front leg) - Rear Uppercut - Lead Uppercut -

Body Opponent Bag Combinations

Diagonal Knee (rear)

- Hook Kick (front) - Straight Right (high)
- Hook Kick (front) - Straight Right (low)
- Hook Kick (front) - Straight Right (high) - Lead Hook (high)
- Hook Kick (front) - Straight Right (high) - Lead Hook (low)
- Hook Kick (front) - Rear Hook (high) - Rear Hook (high)
- Hook Kick (front) - Rear Hook (low) - Rear Hook (low)
- Hook Kick (front) - Rear Hook (high) - Rear Hook (low)
- Hook Kick (front) - Rear Hook (low) - Rear Hook (high)
- Side Kick (front) - Jab - Straight Right
- Side Kick (front) - Jab - Straight Right - Lead Hook
- Side Kick (front) - Straight Right
- Side Kick (front) - Straight Right - Lead Straight
- Side Kick (front) - Straight Right - Horizontal Elbow (front)
- Side Kick (front) - Straight Right - Horizontal Elbow (front) - Horizontal Elbow (rear)
- Side Kick (front) - Straight Right - Hook Kick (front)
- Side Kick (front) - Diagonal Knee (rear)
- Side Kick (front) - Diagonal Knee (rear) - Horizontal Elbow (front)

More Body Opponent Bag Workout Tips

- Before you begin your workout program, make certain that you have been cleared by your doctor. Since there is always some risk involved in training and because each person is unique, it is important that before beginning any type of training program, you should have a complete physical examination by your physician.

- Before hitting the bag, always warm up with some light stretching and calisthenics.

- Always start your first round on the bag with light punches and kicks. Never go all out in the beginning of your workout session.

- When hitting the bag, never sacrifice proper technique for power or speed.

- Always throw your punching or kicking techniques from a good fighting stance.

- Don't chew gum when working out on the bag.

- Avoid wearing watches and jewelry when training.

- Consider shadow boxing with light dumbbells to strengthen your arm and shoulders for bag work.

- Never hold your breath. Remember to exhale with the delivery of every technique.

- Before you invest your time and money in a body opponent bag program, it's important to first define your goals. What do you hope to accomplish by training on the bag? For example, do you want to get in better shape? Build up your confidence? Become a pro fighter? Enter a mixed martial arts competition?

- Be cognizant of your distance from the bag always. Stand too close when punching the bag will result in a "pushing effect" while standing too far will just cause the punch to simply glance the target.

- Avoid the habit of tapping your gloves together before delivering a punch on the bag.

- If you don't know the proper way to throw a punch or kick, get instruction from a qualified coach or instructor.

- Avoid locking out your elbows when punching the bag.

- Be mobile when working out on the bag, avoid the tendency to just stand and punch.

- Avoid premature exhaustion by pacing yourself during your bag workouts.

- The BOB doesn't hit back, so be aware of your own target openings and vulnerabilities when hitting the bag.

- Never let children play or swing from the bag.

- Remember to maintain your balance always when punching the bag - never sacrifice your balance for power.

- The BOB can be unforgiving on your body and will certainly test the structural integrity of you punches and blows. Please remember to keep your wrists straight when your fists hit the bag. Learn to gradually build up the force of your blows - a beginner's wrists are generally too weak to accommodate full force strikes on the bag.

- When using the body opponent bag, learn to relax and avoid unnecessarily tensing your arm and shoulder muscles. Muscular tension will throw off the timing of your punches, retard the speed of your blows, kicks and strikes and most certainly wear you out during your workout.

- Punching bags often cause fighters to "lose their form" when delivering their blows. Try to be constantly aware of your form when hitting the bag or better yet have a training partner, teacher or coach observe you when working out on the bag. Another suggestion is to video tape yourself using the punching bag. This will give you a good idea of what you are doing in your workouts.

- Remember to maintain your balance at all times when punching the bag - never sacrifice your balance for power.

- Avoid bag training two days in a row. Give your body a few days to recover from your last workout.

- To avoid injury or burn out, don't engage in BOB training more than three times per week.

- Get into the habit of regularly inspecting your bag for tears and other signs of wear.

- Avoid the latest gimmicks - Every so often, some cleaver marketing company will come up with a trendy gimmick that can be added to your workouts. Keep your punching bag workouts plain and simple. Beginners should avoid adding hand weights, weighted bag gloves, resistance bands and elevations masks to their workouts.

- While many people use the body opponent bag for boxing, kick boxing and mixed martial arts training, don't forget the BOB is a fantastic tool for developing effective self-defense techniques.

- Remember that BOB training for combat sports is much different from heavy bag training for real world self-defense scenarios.

- Unless you are highly skilled martial artist, do not kick a body opponent bag while bare foot.

- Stay hydrated when working out on the bag. Dehydration can have a real negative effect on your workout, and it can also be dangerous. When working out, always drink plenty of water. Always hydrate before your workout by drinking at least one pint of water. During the summer months, drink more water than usual. Also get into the habit of taking a water bottle with you to your workouts.

- When buying gear, spare no expense. Body opponent bag training is a serious matter, and your training gear should reflect it. Good equipment will provide years of reliable use and enhance your fighting skills.

- Consider working out with music. Actually, your workouts can be dramatically enhanced by training to music. It's my experience that training to fast, rhythmic music works wonders for conditioning training, while hard-driving aggressive rock music works best for proficiency and street training methods.

Avoiding Overtraining & Burnout

Burnout is defined as a negative emotional state acquired by physical overtraining. Some symptoms of burnout include physical illness, boredom, anxiety, disinterest in training, and general sluggish behavior. Whether you are a beginner or expert, you're susceptible to burnout. Here are a few suggestions to help avoid burnout in your training:

- Make your workouts intense but enjoyable.
- Vary your training routine (i.e., hard day/easy day routine).
- Train to different types of music.
- Pace yourself during your workouts - don't try to do it all in one day.
- Listen to your body- if you don't feel up to training, skip a day.
- Work out in different types of environments.
- Use different types of boxing and bag gloves.
- Workout with different training partners.
- Keep accurate records of your training routine.
- Vary the intensity of your training throughout your workout.

Keeping Track of Your Body Opponent Workouts

In order to reap the full benefits of training, you need to keep track of your workouts and monitor your progress. Monitoring your training will give you a wide range of benefits, including:

1. Help determine if you making progress in your training.
2. The ability to effectively alter your training program.
3. Track your rate of progress.
4. Stay interested and motivated.

5. Break through combination plateaus.

Two of the best tools for keeping track of your training progress are: the training journal and video footage. Let's take a look at each one.

The Training Journal

Record keeping is one of the most important and often neglected aspects of training. Try to make it a habit to keep accurate records of your workouts in a personal journal. This type of record keeping is important for some of the following reasons:

- It will help you monitor your progress.
- It will keep you organized.
- It will inspire, motivate and remind you to stick to your goals.
- It helps prevent potential injuries.
- It will help you guard against over training.
- If you are learning new combinations, it accelerates the learning process.
- It gives you valuable training information that can be analyzed.
- It helps you determine which combinations are unproductive.
- It helps you determine which activities are helpful and productive.

When making entries into your journal, don't forget to include some of the following important details:

- The date and time you trained.
- The attribute you are training.
- The types of combinations you performed.

Body Opponent Bag Combinations

- The number or sets, reps you performed for each exercise or drill.

- The number or rounds and minutes per round you performed for each drill or exercise.

- The feelings you experienced before, during, and after your workout.

- Your overall mood.

- Concerns you have about your current training.

- Comments, ideas and observations made by your coach, training partner or instructor.

Videotaping Your Workouts

If you really want to actually see your progress, videotape your workouts. The video will provide you with a more accurate picture of what you are doing in your training. You will be able to observe mistakes and recognize your strengths and weaknesses. The video footage will also motivate you to train harder. Remember to date each videotape or video clip; later on you will be able to compare and see marked improvements in your workout performance.

Body Opponent Bag Maintenance

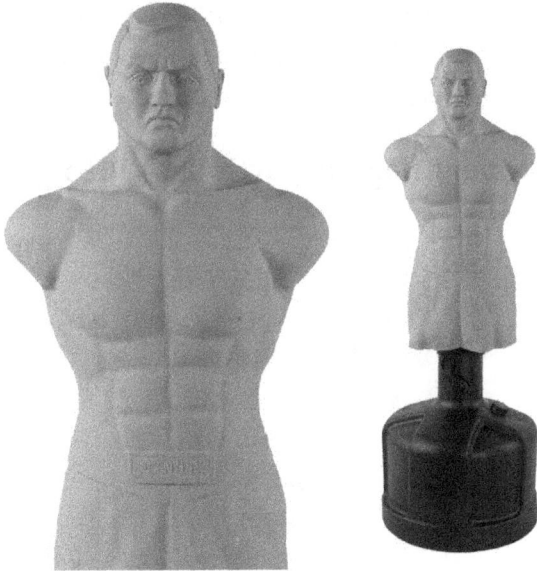

The body opponent bag is a low maintenance piece of equipment that will last for years if you take care of it. What follows are a few tips to help keep it in good working condition.

1. Use soap and water to clean the torso, stem and base of the bag. Avoid using strong detergents and cleaners.

2. If the skin of the mannequin develops a tear, try repairing it with vinyl adhesive that is available at most hardware stores.

3. Avoid exposing the body opponent bag to extreme temperatures.

4. Keep the torso away from direct sunlight for extended periods of time.

5. If you must keep the bag outdoors, keep it away from the elements such as tree sap, or bird droppings. Also, consider placing a vinyl tarp over it when it's not in use.

6. Always keep the base of the bag on a flat level surface.

Body Opponent Bag Resources

If you wish to explore additional information about Body Opponent Bag training, I encourage you to check out the following video and book resources.

Body Opponent Bag Instructional Video

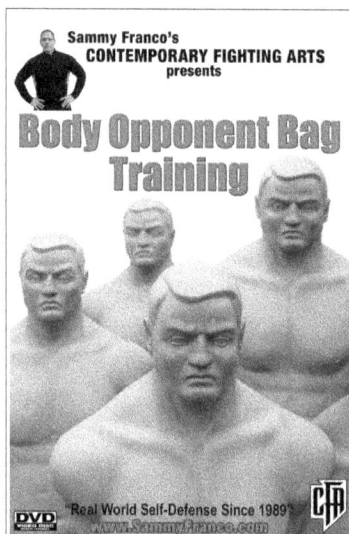

The Body Opponent Bag Training video teaches you sixteen unique Body Opponent Bag workouts. Regardless of your martial art style or self-defense system, you can achieve significant improvement in your self-defense skills when performing these cutting edge routines. Ideal for self-defense, martial artists of all styles and systems, mixed martial artists training and fitness and exercises enthusiasts of all ages.

The Complete Body Opponent Bag Book

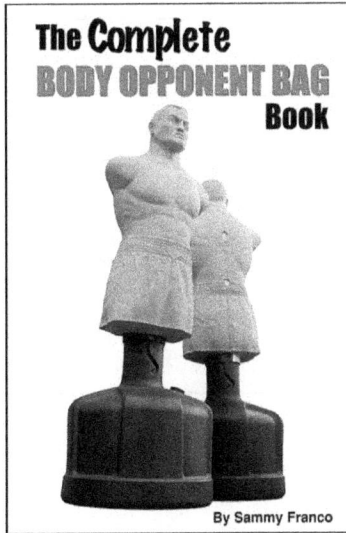

This one-of-a-kind book teaches you the many hidden training features of the body opponent bag (BOB) that will improve your self-defense skills and accelerate your fitness and conditioning.

With detailed photographs, step-by-step instructions, and dozens of unique "out of the box" workout routines, The Complete Body Opponent Bag Book is the authoritative resource for mastering this lifelike punching bag.

Whether you are a beginner, intermediate or advanced practitioner, The Complete Body Opponent Bag Book is an invaluable training resource that you'll refer to again and again.

NOTES

_____

_____

_____

_____

_____

_____

_____

_____

_____

_____

_____

_____

_____

_____

_____

Glossary

The following terms are defined in the context of Contemporary Fighting Arts and its related concepts. In many instances, the definitions bear little resemblance to those found in a standard dictionary.

A

accuracy—The precise or exact projection of force. Accuracy is also defined as the ability to execute a combative movement with precision and exactness.

adaptability—The ability to physically and psychologically adjust to new or different conditions or circumstances of combat.

advanced first-strike tools—Offensive techniques that are specifically used when confronted with multiple opponents.

aerobic exercise—Literally, "with air." Exercise that elevates the heart rate to a training level for a prolonged period of time, usually 30 minutes.

affective preparedness – One of the three components of preparedness. Affective preparedness means being emotionally, philosophically, and spiritually prepared for the strains of combat. See cognitive preparedness and psychomotor preparedness.

aggression—Hostile and injurious behavior directed toward a person.

aggressive response—One of the three possible counters when assaulted by a grab, choke, or hold from a standing position. Aggressive response requires you to counter the enemy with destructive blows and strikes. See moderate response and passive response.

aggressive hand positioning—Placement of hands so as to imply aggressive or hostile intentions.

agility—An attribute of combat. One's ability to move his or her body quickly and gracefully.

amalgamation—A scientific process of uniting or merging.

ambidextrous—The ability to perform with equal facility on both the right and left sides of the body.

anabolic steroids – synthetic chemical compounds that resemble the male sex hormone testosterone. This performance-enhancing drug is known to increase lean muscle mass, strength, and endurance.

analysis and integration—One of the five elements of CFA's mental component. This is the painstaking process of breaking down various elements, concepts, sciences, and disciplines into their atomic parts, and then methodically and strategically analyzing, experimenting, and drastically modifying the information so that it fulfills three combative requirements: efficiency, effectiveness, and safety. Only then is it finally integrated into the CFA system.

anatomical striking targets—The various anatomical body targets that can be struck and which are especially vulnerable to potential harm. They include: the eyes, temple, nose, chin, back of neck, front of neck, solar plexus, ribs, groin, thighs, knees, shins, and instep.

anchoring – The strategic process of trapping the assailant's neck or limb in order to control the range of engagement during razing.

assailant—A person who threatens or attacks another person.

assault—The threat or willful attempt to inflict injury upon the person of another.

assault and battery—The unlawful touching of another person without justification.

assessment—The process of rapidly gathering, analyzing, and accurately evaluating information in terms of threat and danger. You can assess people, places, actions, and objects.

attack—Offensive action designed to physically control, injure, or kill another person.

attack by combination (ABC) - One of the five methods of attack. See compound attack.

attack by drawing (ABD) - One of the five methods of attack. A method of attack predicated on counterattack.

attitude—One of the three factors that determine who wins a street fight. Attitude means being emotionally, philosophically, and spiritually liberated from societal and religious mores. See skills and knowledge.

attributes of combat—The physical, mental, and spiritual qualities that enhance combat skills and tactics.

awareness—Perception or knowledge of people, places, actions, and objects. (In CFA, there are three categories of tactical awareness: criminal awareness, situational awareness, and self-awareness.)

B

balance—One's ability to maintain equilibrium while stationary or moving.

blading the body—Strategically positioning your body at a 45-degree angle.

blitz and disengage—A style of sparring whereby a fighter moves into a range of combat, unleashes a strategic compound attack, and then quickly disengages to a safe distance. Of all sparring methodologies, the blitz and disengage most closely resembles a real street fight.

block—A defensive tool designed to intercept the assailant's attack by placing a non-vital target between the assailant's strike and your vital body target.

body composition—The ratio of fat to lean body tissue.

body language—Nonverbal communication through posture, gestures, and facial expressions.

body mechanics—Technically precise body movement during the execution of a body weapon, defensive technique, or other fighting maneuver.

body tackle – A tackle that occurs when your opponent haphazardly rushes forward and plows his body into yours.

body weapon—Also known as a tool, one of the various body parts that can be used to strike or otherwise injure or kill a criminal assailant.

burn out—A negative emotional state acquired by physically over- training. Some symptoms include: illness, boredom, anxiety, disinterest in training, and general sluggishness.

C

cadence—Coordinating tempo and rhythm to establish a timing pattern of movement.

cardiorespiratory conditioning—The component of physical fitness that deals with the heart, lungs, and circulatory system.

centerline—An imaginary vertical line that divides your body in half and which contains many of your vital anatomical targets.

choke holds—Holds that impair the flow of blood or oxygen to the brain.

circular movements—Movements that follow the direction of a curve.

close-quarter combat—One of the three ranges of knife and

bludgeon combat. At this distance, you can strike, slash, or stab your assailant with a variety of close-quarter techniques.

cognitive development—One of the five elements of CFA's mental component. The process of developing and enhancing your fighting skills through specific mental exercises and techniques. See analysis and integration, killer instinct, philosophy, and strategic/tactical development.

cognitive exercises—Various mental exercises used to enhance fighting skills and tactics.

cognitive preparedness – One of the three components of preparedness. Cognitive preparedness means being equipped with the strategic concepts, principles, and general knowledge of combat. See affective preparedness and psychomotor preparedness.

combat-oriented training—Training that is specifically related to the harsh realities of both armed and unarmed combat. See ritual-oriented training and sport-oriented training.

combative arts—The various arts of war. See martial arts.

combative attributes—See attributes of combat.

combative fitness—A state characterized by cardiorespiratory and muscular/skeletal conditioning, as well as proper body composition.

combative mentality—Also known as the killer instinct, this is a combative state of mind necessary for fighting. See killer instinct.

combat ranges—The various ranges of unarmed combat.

combative utility—The quality of condition of being combatively useful.

combination(s)—See compound attack.

common peroneal nerve—A pressure point area located approximately four to six inches above the knee on the midline of the outside of the thigh.

composure—A combative attribute. Composure is a quiet and focused mind-set that enables you to acquire your combative agenda.

compound attack—One of the five conventional methods of attack. Two or more body weapons launched in strategic succession whereby the fighter overwhelms his assailant with a flurry of full speed, full-force blows.

conditioning training—A CFA training methodology requiring the practitioner to deliver a variety of offensive and defensive combinations for a 4-minute period. See proficiency training and street training.

contact evasion—Physically moving or manipulating your body to avoid being tackled by the adversary.

Contemporary Fighting Arts—A modern martial art and self-defense system made up of three parts: physical, mental, and spiritual.

conventional ground-fighting tools—Specific ground-fighting techniques designed to control, restrain, and temporarily incapacitate your adversary. Some conventional ground fighting tactics include: submission holds, locks, certain choking techniques, and specific striking techniques.

coordination—A physical attribute characterized by the ability to perform a technique or movement with efficiency, balance, and accuracy.

counterattack—Offensive action made to counter an assailant's initial attack.

courage—A combative attribute. The state of mind and spirit that enables a fighter to face danger and vicissitudes with confidence, resolution, and bravery.

creatine monohydrate—A tasteless and odorless white powder that mimics some of the effects of anabolic steroids. Creatine is a safe body-building product that can benefit anyone who wants to increase their strength, endurance, and lean muscle mass.

criminal awareness—One of the three categories of CFA awareness. It involves a general understanding and knowledge of the nature and dynamics of a criminal's motivations, mentalities, methods, and capabilities to perpetrate violent crime. See situational awareness and self-awareness.

criminal justice—The study of criminal law and the procedures associated with its enforcement.

criminology—The scientific study of crime and criminals.

cross-stepping—The process of crossing one foot in front of or behind the other when moving.

crushing tactics—Nuclear grappling-range techniques designed to crush the assailant's anatomical targets.

D

deadly force—Weapons or techniques that may result in unconsciousness, permanent disfigurement, or death.

deception—A combative attribute. A stratagem whereby you delude your assailant.

decisiveness—A combative attribute. The ability to follow a tactical course of action that is unwavering and focused.

defense—The ability to strategically thwart an assailant's attack (armed or unarmed).

defensive flow—A progression of continuous defensive responses.

defensive mentality—A defensive mind-set.

defensive reaction time—The elapsed time between an assailant's physical attack and your defensive response to that attack. See offensive reaction time.

demeanor—A person's outward behavior. One of the essential factors to consider when assessing a threatening individual.

diet—A lifestyle of healthy eating.

disingenuous vocalization—The strategic and deceptive utilization of words to successfully launch a preemptive strike at your adversary.

distancing—The ability to quickly understand spatial relationships and how they relate to combat.

distractionary tactics—Various verbal and physical tactics designed to distract your adversary.

double-end bag—A small leather ball hung from the ceiling and anchored to the floor with bungee cord. It helps develop striking accuracy, speed, timing, eye-hand coordination, footwork and overall defensive skills.

double-leg takedown—A takedown that occurs when your opponent shoots for both of your legs to force you to the ground.

E

ectomorph—One of the three somatotypes. A body type characterized by a high degree of slenderness, angularity, and fragility. See endomorph and mesomorph.

effectiveness—One of the three criteria for a CFA body weapon, technique, tactic, or maneuver. It means the ability to produce a desired effect. See efficiency and safety.

efficiency—One of the three criteria for a CFA body weapon, technique, tactic, or maneuver. It means the ability to reach an objective quickly and economically. See effectiveness and safety.

emotionless—A combative attribute. Being temporarily devoid of human feeling.

endomorph—One of the three somatotypes. A body type characterized by a high degree of roundness, softness, and body fat. See ectomorph and mesomorph.

evasion—A defensive maneuver that allows you to strategically maneuver your body away from the assailant's strike.

evasive sidestepping—Evasive footwork where the practitioner moves to either the right or left side.

evasiveness—A combative attribute. The ability to avoid threat or danger.

excessive force—An amount of force that exceeds the need for a particular event and is unjustified in the eyes of the law.

experimentation—The painstaking process of testing a combative hypothesis or theory.

explosiveness—A combative attribute that is characterized by a sudden outburst of violent energy.

F

fear—A strong and unpleasant emotion caused by the anticipation or awareness of threat or danger. There are three stages of fear in order of intensity: fright, panic, and terror. See fright, panic, and terror.

feeder—A skilled technician who manipulates the focus mitts.

femoral nerve—A pressure point area located approximately 6 inches above the knee on the inside of the thigh.

fighting stance—Any one of the stances used in CFA's system. A strategic posture you can assume when face-to-face with an unarmed assailant(s). The fighting stance is generally used after you have launched your first-strike tool.

fight-or-flight syndrome—A response of the sympathetic nervous system to a fearful and threatening situation, during which it prepares your body to either fight or flee from the perceived danger.

finesse—A combative attribute. The ability to skillfully execute a movement or a series of movements with grace and refinement.

first strike—Proactive force used to interrupt the initial stages of an assault before it becomes a self-defense situation.

first-strike principle—A CFA principle that states that when physical danger is imminent and you have no other tactical option but to fight back, you should strike first, strike fast, and strike with authority and keep the pressure on.

first-strike stance—One of the stances used in CFA's system. A strategic posture used prior to initiating a first strike.

first-strike tools—Specific offensive tools designed to initiate a preemptive strike against your adversary.

fisted blows – Hand blows delivered with a clenched fist.

five tactical options – The five strategic responses you can make in a self-defense situation, listed in order of increasing level of resistance: comply, escape, de-escalate, assert, and fight back.

flexibility—The muscles' ability to move through maximum natural ranges. See muscular/skeletal conditioning.

focus mitts—Durable leather hand mitts used to develop and sharpen offensive and defensive skills.

footwork—Quick, economical steps performed on the balls of the feet while you are relaxed, alert, and balanced. Footwork is structured around four general movements: forward, backward, right, and left.

fractal tool—Offensive or defensive tools that can be used in more than one combat range.

fright—The first stage of fear; quick and sudden fear. See panic and terror.

full Beat – One of the four beat classifications in the Widow Maker Program. The full beat strike has a complete initiation and retraction phase.

G

going postal - a slang term referring to a person who suddenly and unexpectedly attacks you with an explosive and frenzied flurry of blows. Also known as postal attack.

grappling range—One of the three ranges of unarmed combat. Grappling range is the closest distance of unarmed combat from which you can employ a wide variety of close-quarter tools and techniques. The grappling range of unarmed combat is also divided into two planes: vertical (standing) and horizontal (ground fighting). See kicking range and punching range.

grappling-range tools—The various body tools and techniques that are employed in the grappling range of unarmed combat, including head butts; biting, tearing, clawing, crushing, and gouging tactics; foot stomps, horizontal, vertical, and diagonal elbow strikes, vertical and diagonal knee strikes, chokes, strangles, joint locks, and holds. See punching range tools and kicking range tools.

ground fighting—Also known as the horizontal grappling plane, this is fighting that takes place on the ground.

guard—Also known as the hand guard, this refers to a fighter's hand positioning.

guard position—Also known as leg guard or scissors hold, this is a ground-fighting position in which a fighter is on his back holding his opponent between his legs.

H

half beat – One of the four beat classifications in the Widow Maker Program. The half beat strike is delivered through the retraction phase of the proceeding strike.

hand immobilization attack (HIA) - One of the five methods of attack. A method of attack whereby the practitioner traps his opponent's limb or limbs in order to execute an offense attack of his own.

hand positioning—See guard.

hand wraps—Long strips of cotton that are wrapped around the hands and wrists for greater protection.

haymaker—A wild and telegraphed swing of the arms executed by an unskilled fighter.

head-hunter—A fighter who primarily attacks the head.

heavy bag—A large cylindrical bag used to develop kicking, punching, or striking power.

high-line kick—One of the two different classifications of a kick. A kick that is directed to targets above an assailant's waist level. See low-line kick.

hip fusing—A full-contact drill that teaches a fighter to "stand his ground" and overcome the fear of exchanging blows with a stronger opponent. This exercise is performed by connecting two fighters with a 3-foot chain, forcing them to fight in the punching range of unarmed combat.

histrionics—The field of theatrics or acting.

hook kick—A circular kick that can be delivered in both kicking and punching ranges.

hook punch—A circular punch that can be delivered in both the punching and grappling ranges.

I

impact power—Destructive force generated by mass and velocity.

impact training—A training exercise that develops pain tolerance.

incapacitate—To disable an assailant by rendering him unconscious or damaging his bones, joints, or organs.

initiative—Making the first offensive move in combat.

inside position—The area between the opponent's arms, where he has the greatest amount of control.

intent—One of the essential factors to consider when assessing a threatening individual. The assailant's purpose or motive. See demeanor, positioning, range, and weapon capability.

intuition—The innate ability to know or sense something without the use of rational thought.

J

jeet kune do (JKD) - "Way of the intercepting fist." Bruce Lee's approach to the martial arts, which includes his innovative concepts, theories, methodologies, and philosophies.

jersey Pull – Strategically pulling the assailant's shirt or jacket over his head as he disengages from the clinch position.

joint lock—A grappling-range technique that immobilizes the assailant's joint.

K

kick—A sudden, forceful strike with the foot.

kicking range—One of the three ranges of unarmed combat. Kicking range is the furthest distance of unarmed combat wherein you use your legs to strike an assailant. See grappling range and punching range.

kicking-range tools—The various body weapons employed in the kicking range of unarmed combat, including side kicks, push kicks, hook kicks, and vertical kicks.

killer instinct—A cold, primal mentality that surges to your consciousness and turns you into a vicious fighter.

kinesics—The study of nonlinguistic body movement communications. (For example, eye movement, shrugs, or facial gestures.)

kinesiology—The study of principles and mechanics of human movement.

kinesthetic perception—The ability to accurately feel your body during the execution of a particular movement.

knowledge—One of the three factors that determine who will win a street fight. Knowledge means knowing and understanding how to fight. See skills and attitude.

L

lead side -The side of the body that faces an assailant.

leg guard—See guard position.

linear movement—Movements that follow the path of a straight line.

low-maintenance tool—Offensive and defensive tools that require the least amount of training and practice to maintain proficiency. Low maintenance tools generally do not require preliminary stretching.

low-line kick—One of the two different classifications of a kick. A kick that is directed to targets below the assailant's waist level. (See high-line kick.)

lock—See joint lock.

M

maneuver—To manipulate into a strategically desired position.

MAP—An acronym that stands for moderate, aggressive, passive. MAP provides the practitioner with three possible responses to various grabs, chokes, and holds that occur from a standing position. See aggressive response, moderate response, and passive response.

martial arts—The "arts of war."

masking—The process of concealing your true feelings from your opponent by manipulating and managing your body language.

mechanics—(See body mechanics.)

mental attributes—The various cognitive qualities that enhance your fighting skills.

mental component—One of the three vital components of the CFA system. The mental component includes the cerebral aspects of fighting including the killer instinct, strategic and tactical development, analysis and integration, philosophy, and cognitive development. See physical component and spiritual component.

mesomorph—One of the three somatotypes. A body type classified by a high degree of muscularity and strength. The mesomorph possesses the ideal physique for unarmed combat. See ectomorph and endomorph.

mobility—A combative attribute. The ability to move your body quickly and freely while balanced. See footwork.

moderate response—One of the three possible counters when assaulted by a grab, choke, or hold from a standing position. Moderate response requires you to counter your opponent with a control and restraint (submission hold). See aggressive response and passive response.

modern martial art—A pragmatic combat art that has evolved to meet the demands and characteristics of the present time.

mounted position—A dominant ground-fighting position where a fighter straddles his opponent.

muscular endurance—The muscles' ability to perform the same motion or task repeatedly for a prolonged period of time.

muscular flexibility—The muscles' ability to move through maximum natural ranges.

muscular strength—The maximum force that can be exerted by a particular muscle or muscle group against resistance.

muscular/skeletal conditioning—An element of physical fitness that entails muscular strength, endurance, and flexibility.

N

naked choke—A throat choke executed from the chest to back position. This secure choke is executed with two hands and it can be performed while standing, kneeling, and ground fighting with the opponent.

neck crush – A powerful pain compliance technique used when the adversary buries his head in your chest to avoid being razed.

neutralize—See incapacitate.

neutral zone—The distance outside the kicking range at which neither the practitioner nor the assailant can touch the other.

nonaggressive physiology—Strategic body language used prior to initiating a first strike.

nontelegraphic movement—Body mechanics or movements that do not inform an assailant of your intentions.

nuclear ground-fighting tools—Specific grappling range tools designed to inflict immediate and irreversible damage. Nuclear tools and tactics include biting tactics, tearing tactics, crushing tactics, continuous choking tactics, gouging techniques, raking tactics, and all striking techniques.

O

offense—The armed and unarmed means and methods of attacking a criminal assailant.

offensive flow—Continuous offensive movements (kicks, blows, and strikes) with unbroken continuity that ultimately neutralize or terminate the opponent. See compound attack.

offensive reaction time—The elapsed time between target selection and target impaction.

one-mindedness—A state of deep concentration wherein you are free from all distractions (internal and external).

ostrich defense—One of the biggest mistakes one can make when defending against an opponent. This is when the practitioner looks away from that which he fears (punches, kicks, and strikes). His mentality is, "If I can't see it, it can't hurt me."

P

pain tolerance—Your ability to physically and psychologically withstand pain.

panic—The second stage of fear; overpowering fear. See fright and terror.

parry—A defensive technique: a quick, forceful slap that redirects an assailant's linear attack. There are two types of parries: horizontal and vertical.

passive response—One of the three possible counters when assaulted by a grab, choke, or hold from a standing position. Passive response requires you to nullify the assault without injuring your adversary. See aggressive response and moderate response.

patience—A combative attribute. The ability to endure and tolerate difficulty.

perception—Interpretation of vital information acquired from your senses when faced with a potentially threatening situation.

philosophical resolution—The act of analyzing and answering various questions concerning the use of violence in defense of yourself and others.

philosophy—One of the five aspects of CFA's mental component. A deep state of introspection whereby you methodically resolve critical questions concerning the use of force in defense of yourself or others.

physical attributes—The numerous physical qualities that enhance your combative skills and abilities.

physical component—One of the three vital components of the CFA system. The physical component includes the physical aspects of fighting, such as physical fitness, weapon/technique mastery, and combative attributes. See mental component and spiritual component.

physical conditioning—See combative fitness.

physical fitness—See combative fitness.

positional asphyxia—The arrangement, placement, or positioning of your opponent's body in such a way as to interrupt your breathing and cause unconsciousness or possibly death.

positioning—The spatial relationship of the assailant to the assailed person in terms of target exposure, escape, angle of attack, and various other strategic considerations.

postal attack - see going postal.

power—A physical attribute of armed and unarmed combat. The amount of force you can generate when striking an anatomical target.

power generators—Specific points on your body that generate impact power. There are three anatomical power generators: shoulders, hips, and feet.

precision—See accuracy.

preemptive strike—See first strike.

premise—An axiom, concept, rule, or any other valid reason to modify or go beyond that which has been established.

preparedness—A state of being ready for combat. There are three components of preparedness: affective preparedness, cognitive preparedness, and psychomotor preparedness.

probable reaction dynamics - The opponent's anticipated or predicted movements or actions during both armed and unarmed combat.

proficiency training—A CFA training methodology requiring the practitioner to execute a specific body weapon, technique, maneuver, or tactic over and over for a prescribed number of repetitions. See conditioning training and street training.

progressive indirect attack (PIA) – One of the five methods of attack. A progressive method of attack whereby the initial tool or technique is designed to set the opponent up for follow-up blows.

proxemics—The study of the nature and effect of man's personal space.

proximity—The ability to maintain a strategically safe distance from a threatening individual.

pseudospeciation—A combative attribute. The tendency to assign subhuman and inferior qualities to a threatening assailant.

psychological conditioning—The process of conditioning the mind for the horrors and rigors of real combat.

psychomotor preparedness—One of the three components of preparedness. Psychomotor preparedness means possessing all of the physical skills and attributes necessary to defeat a formidable adversary. See affective preparedness and cognitive preparedness.

punch—A quick, forceful strike of the fists.

punching range—One of the three ranges of unarmed combat. Punching range is the mid range of unarmed combat from which the fighter uses his hands to strike his assailant. See kicking range and grappling range.

punching-range tools—The various body weapons that are employed in the punching range of unarmed combat, including finger jabs, palm-heel strikes, rear cross, knife-hand strikes, horizontal and shovel hooks, uppercuts, and hammer-fist strikes. See grappling-range tools and kicking-range tools.

Q

qualities of combat—See attributes of combat.

quarter beat - One of the four beat classifications of the Widow Maker Program. Quarter beat strikes never break contact with the assailant's face. Quarter beat strikes are primarily responsible for creating the psychological panic and trauma when Razing.

R

range—The spatial relationship between a fighter and a threatening assailant.

range deficiency—The inability to effectively fight and defend in all ranges of combat (armed and unarmed).

range manipulation—A combative attribute. The strategic manipulation of combat ranges.

range proficiency—A combative attribute. The ability to effectively fight and defend in all ranges of combat (armed and unarmed).

ranges of engagement—See combat ranges.

ranges of unarmed combat—The three distances (kicking range, punching range, and grappling range) a fighter might physically engage with an assailant while involved in unarmed combat.

raze – To level, demolish or obliterate.

razer – One who performs the Razing methodology.

razing – The second phase of the Widow Maker Program. A series of vicious close quarter techniques designed to physically and psychologically extirpate a criminal attacker.

razing amplifier - a technique, tactic or procedure that magnifies the destructiveness of your razing technique.

reaction dynamics—see probable reaction dynamics.

reaction time—The elapsed time between a stimulus and the response to that particular stimulus. See offensive reaction time and defensive reaction time.

rear cross—A straight punch delivered from the rear hand that crosses from right to left (if in a left stance) or left to right (if in a right stance).

rear side—The side of the body furthest from the assailant. See lead side.

reasonable force—That degree of force which is not excessive for a particular event and which is appropriate in protecting yourself or others.

refinement—The strategic and methodical process of improving or perfecting.

relocation principle—Also known as relocating, this is a street-fighting tactic that requires you to immediately move to a new location (usually by flanking your adversary) after delivering a compound attack.

repetition—Performing a single movement, exercise, strike, or action continuously for a specific period.

research—A scientific investigation or inquiry.

rhythm—Movements characterized by the natural ebb and flow of related elements.

ritual-oriented training—Formalized training that is conducted without intrinsic purpose. See combat-oriented training and sport-oriented training.

S

safety—One of the three criteria for a CFA body weapon, technique, maneuver, or tactic. It means that the tool, technique, maneuver or tactic provides the least amount of danger and risk for the practitioner. See efficiency and effectiveness.

scissors hold—See guard position.

scorching – Quickly and inconspicuously applying oleoresin capsicum (hot pepper extract) on your fingertips and then razing your adversary.

self-awareness—One of the three categories of CFA awareness. Knowing and understanding yourself. This includes aspects of yourself which may provoke criminal violence and which will promote a proper and strong reaction to an attack. See criminal awareness and situational awareness.

self-confidence—Having trust and faith in yourself.

self-enlightenment—The state of knowing your capabilities, limitations, character traits, feelings, general attributes, and motivations. See self-awareness.

set—A term used to describe a grouping of repetitions.

shadow fighting—A CFA training exercise used to develop and refine your tools, techniques, and attributes of armed and unarmed combat.

sharking – A counter attack technique that is used when your adversary grabs your razing hand.

shielding wedge - a defensive maneuver used to counter an unarmed postal attack.

simple direct attack (SDA) – One of the five methods of attack. A method of attack whereby the practitioner delivers a solitary offenses tool or technique. It may involve a series of discrete probes or one swift, powerful strike aimed at terminating the encounter.

situational awareness—One of the three categories of CFA awareness. A state of being totally alert to your immediate surroundings, including people, places, objects, and actions. (See criminal awareness and self-awareness.)

skeletal alignment—The proper alignment or arrangement of your body. Skeletal alignment maximizes the structural integrity of striking tools.

skills—One of the three factors that determine who will win a street fight. Skills refers to psychomotor proficiency with the tools and techniques of combat. See Attitude and Knowledge.

slipping—A defensive maneuver that permits you to avoid an assailant's linear blow without stepping out of range. Slipping can be accomplished by quickly snapping the head and upper torso sideways (right or left) to avoid the blow.

snap back—A defensive maneuver that permits you to avoid an assailant's linear and circular blows without stepping out of range. The snap back can be accomplished by quickly snapping the head backward to avoid the assailant's blow.

somatotypes—A method of classifying human body types or builds into three different categories: endomorph, mesomorph, and ectomorph. See endomorph, mesomorph, and ectomorph.

sparring—A training exercise where two or more fighters fight each other while wearing protective equipment.

speed—A physical attribute of armed and unarmed combat. The rate or a measure of the rapid rate of motion.

spiritual component—One of the three vital components of the CFA system. The spiritual component includes the metaphysical issues and aspects of existence. See physical component and mental component.

sport-oriented training—Training that is geared for competition and governed by a set of rules. See combat-oriented training and ritual-oriented training.

sprawling—A grappling technique used to counter a double- or single-leg takedown.

square off—To be face-to-face with a hostile or threatening assailant who is about to attack you.

stance—One of the many strategic postures you assume prior to or during armed or unarmed combat.

stick fighting—Fighting that takes place with either one or two sticks.

strategic positioning—Tactically positioning yourself to either escape, move behind a barrier, or use a makeshift weapon.

strategic/tactical development—One of the five elements of CFA's mental component.

strategy—A carefully planned method of achieving your goal of engaging an assailant under advantageous conditions.

street fight—A spontaneous and violent confrontation between two or more individuals wherein no rules apply.

street fighter—An unorthodox combatant who has no formal training. His combative skills and tactics are usually developed in the street by the process of trial and error.

street training—A CFA training methodology requiring the practitioner to deliver explosive compound attacks for 10 to 20 seconds. See condition ng training and proficiency training.

strength training—The process of developing muscular strength through systematic application of progressive resistance.

striking art—A combat art that relies predominantly on striking techniques to neutralize or terminate a criminal attacker.

striking shield—A rectangular shield constructed of foam and vinyl used to develop power in your kicks, punches, and strikes.

striking tool—A natural body weapon that impacts with the assailant's anatomical target.

strong side—The strongest and most coordinated side of your body.

structure—A definite and organized pattern.

style—The distinct manner in which a fighter executes or performs his combat skills.

stylistic integration—The purposeful and scientific collection of tools and techniques from various disciplines, which are strategically integrated and dramatically altered to meet three essential criteria: efficiency, effectiveness, and combative safety.

submission holds—Also known as control and restraint techniques, many of these locks and holds create sufficient pain to cause the adversary to submit.

system—The unification of principles, philosophies, rules, strategies, methodologies, tools, and techniques of a particular method of combat.

T

tactic—The skill of using the available means to achieve an end.

target awareness—A combative attribute that encompasses five strategic principles: target orientation, target recognition, target selection, target impaction, and target exploitation.

target exploitation—A combative attribute. The strategic maximization of your assailant's reaction dynamics during a fight. Target exploitation can be applied in both armed and unarmed encounters.

target impaction—The successful striking of the appropriate anatomical target.

target orientation—A combative attribute. Having a workable knowledge of the assailant's anatomical targets.

target recognition—The ability to immediately recognize appropriate anatomical targets during an emergency self-defense situation.

target selection—The process of mentally selecting the appropriate anatomical target for your self-defense situation. This is predicated on certain factors, including proper force response, assailant's positioning, and range.

target stare—A form of telegraphing in which you stare at the anatomical target you intend to strike.

target zones—The three areas in which an assailant's anatomical targets are located. (See zone one, zone two and zone three.)

technique—A systematic procedure by which a task is accomplished.

telegraphic cognizance—A combative attribute. The ability to recognize both verbal and non-verbal signs of aggression or assault.

telegraphing—Unintentionally making your intentions known to your adversary.

tempo—The speed or rate at which you speak.

terminate—To kill.

terror—The third stage of fear; defined as overpowering fear. See fright and panic.

timing—A physical and mental attribute of armed and unarmed combat. Your ability to execute a movement at the optimum moment.

tone—The overall quality or character of your voice.

tool—See body weapon.

traditional martial arts—Any martial art that fails to evolve and change to meet the demands and characteristics of its present environment.

traditional style/system—See traditional martial arts.

training drills—The various exercises and drills aimed at perfecting combat skills, attributes, and tactics.

trap and tuck – A counter move technique used when the adversary attempts to raze you during your quarter beat assault.

U

unified mind—A mind free and clear of distractions and focused on the combative situation.

use of force response—A combative attribute. Selecting the appropriate level of force for a particular emergency self-defense situation.

V

viciousness—A combative attribute. The propensity to be extremely violent and destructive often characterized by intense savagery.

violence—The intentional utilization of physical force to coerce, injure, cripple, or kill.

visualization—Also known as mental visualization or mental imagery. The purposeful formation of mental images and scenarios in the mind's eye.

W

warm-up—A series of mild exercises, stretches, and movements designed to prepare you for more intense exercise.

weak side—The weaker and more uncoordinated side of your body.

weapon and technique mastery—A component of CFA's physical component. The kinesthetic and psychomotor development of a weapon or combative technique.

weapon capability—An assailant's ability to use and attack with a particular weapon.

webbing - The first phase of the Widow Maker Program. Webbing is a two hand strike delivered to the assailant's chin. It is called Webbing because your hands resemble a large web that wraps around the enemy's face.

widow maker – One who makes widows by destroying husbands.

widow maker program – A CFA combat program specifically designed to teach the law abiding citizen how to use extreme force when faced with immediate threat of unlawful deadly criminal attack. The Widow Maker program is divided into two phases or methodologies: Webbing and Razing.

Y

yell—A loud and aggressive scream or shout used for various strategic reasons.

Z

zero beat – One of the four beat classifications of the Widow Maker, Feral Fighting and Savage Street Fighting Programs. Zero beat strikes are full pressure techniques applied to a specific target until it completely ruptures. They include gouging, crushing, biting, and choking techniques.

zone one—Anatomical targets related to your senses, including the eyes, temple, nose, chin, and back of neck.

zone three—Anatomical targets related to your mobility, including thighs, knees, shins, and instep.

zone two—Anatomical targets related to your breathing, including front of neck, solar plexus, ribs, and groin.

Body Opponent Bag Combinations

About Sammy Franco

With over 35 years of experience, Sammy Franco is one of the world's foremost authorities on armed and unarmed self-defense. Highly regarded as a leading innovator in combat sciences, Mr. Franco was one of the premier pioneers in the field of "reality-based" self-defense and martial arts instruction.

Sammy Franco is perhaps best known as the founder and creator of Contemporary Fighting Arts (CFA), a state-of-the-art offensive-based combat system that is specifically designed for real-world self-defense. CFA is a sophisticated and practical system of self-defense, designed specifically to provide efficient and effective methods to avoid, defuse, confront, and neutralize both armed and unarmed attackers.

Sammy Franco has frequently been featured in martial art magazines, newspapers, and appeared on numerous radio and television programs. Mr. Franco has also authored numerous books, magazine articles, and editorials, and has developed a popular library of instructional videos.

Sammy Franco's experience and credibility in the combat sciences is unequaled. One of his many accomplishments in this field includes the fact that he has earned the ranking of a Law Enforcement Master Instructor, and has designed, implemented, and taught officer survival training to the United States Border Patrol (USBP). He has instructed members of the US Secret Service, Military Special Forces, Washington DC Police Department, Montgomery County, Maryland

Knife Fighting Targets

Deputy Sheriffs, and the US Library of Congress Police. Sammy Franco is also a member of the prestigious International Law Enforcement Educators and Trainers Association (ILEETA) as well as the American Society of Law Enforcement Trainers (ASLET) and he is listed in the "Who's Who Director of Law Enforcement Instructors."

Sammy Franco is a nationally certified Law Enforcement Instructor in the following curricula: PR-24 Side-Handle Baton, Police Arrest and Control Procedures, Police Personal Weapons Tactics, Police Power Handcuffing Methods, Police Oleoresin Capsicum Aerosol Training (OCAT), Police Weapon Retention and Disarming Methods, Police Edged Weapon Countermeasures and "Use of Force" Assessment and Response Methods.

Mr. Franco holds a Bachelor of Arts degree in Criminal Justice from the University of Maryland. He is a regularly featured speaker at a number of professional conferences and conducts dynamic and enlightening seminars on numerous aspects of self-defense and combat training.

On a personal level, Sammy Franco is an animal lover, who will go to great lengths to assist and rescue animals. Throughout the years, he's rescued everything from turkey vultures to goats. However, his most treasured moments are always spent with his beloved German Shepherd dogs.

For more information about Mr. Franco and his unique Contemporary Fighting Arts system, you can visit his website at: **ContemporaryFightingArts.com** or follow him on twitter **@RealSammyFranco**

Other Books by Sammy Franco

SPEED BOXING SECRETS
A 21-Day Program to Hitting Faster and Reacting Quicker in Boxing and Mixed Martial Arts
by Sammy Franco

Speed Boxing Secrets: A 21-Day Program to Hitting Faster and Reacting Quicker in Boxing and Mixed Martial Arts is a comprehensive speed acceleration program made for anyone who wants to dramatically improve their fighting speed in a short period of time. When used correctly, this simple speed development program will double your boxing speed in as little as 21 days. 8.5 x 5.5, paperback, photos, illus, 150 pages.

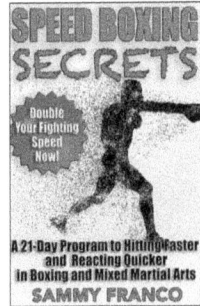

POWER BOXING WORKOUT SECRETS
A 21-Day Program to Becoming a Devastating Knockout Puncher in Boxing and Mixed Martial Arts
by Sammy Franco

Power Boxing Workout Secrets: A 21-Day Program to Becoming a Devastating Knockout Puncher in Boxing and Mixed Martial Arts is a unique power development program made for fighters who want to be champions by dramatically increasing their power and explosiveness in the ring. When used correctly, this comprehensive power program will double your knockout power and fighting explosiveness in as little as 21 days. 8.5 x 5.5, paperback, photos, illus, 160 pages.

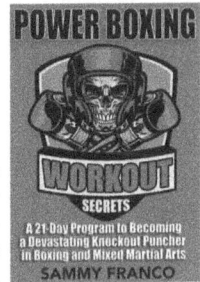

HEAVY BAG TRAINING
For Boxing, Mixed Martial Arts and Self-Defense (Heavy Bag Training Series Book 1)
by Sammy Franco

The heavy bag is one of the oldest and most recognizable pieces of training equipment. It's used by boxers, mixed martial artists, self-defense practitioners, and fitness enthusiasts. Unfortunately, most people don't know how to use the heavy bag correctly. Heavy Bag Training teaches you everything you ever wanted to know about working out on the heavy bag. In this one-of-a-kind book, world-renowned self-defense expert Sammy Franco provides you with the knowledge, skills, and attitude necessary to maximize the training benefits of the bag. 8.5 x 5.5, paperback, photos, illus, 172 pages.

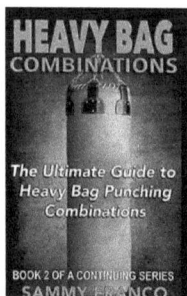

HEAVY BAG COMBINATIONS
The Ultimate Guide to Heavy Bag Punching Combinations
(Heavy Bag Training Series Book 2)
by Sammy Franco

Heavy Bag Combinations is the second book in Sammy Franco's best-selling Heavy Bag Training Series. This unique book is your ultimate guide to mastering devastating heavy bag punching combinations. With over 300+ photographs and detailed step-by-step instructions, Heavy Bag Combinations provides beginner, intermediate and advanced heavy bag workout combinations that will challenge you for the rest of your life! In fact, even the most experienced athlete will advance his fighting skills to the next level and beyond. 8.5 x 5.5, paperback, photos, illus, 248 pages.

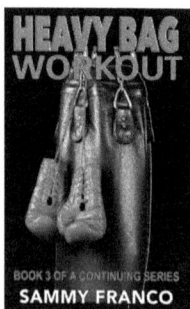

HEAVY BAG WORKOUTS
A Hard-Core Guide to Heavy Bag Workout Routines
(Heavy Bag Training Series Book 3)
by Sammy Franco

Heavy Bag Workout is the third book in Sammy Franco's best-selling Heavy Bag Training Series. This unique book features over two dozen "out of the box" heavy bag workout routines that will maximize your fighting skills for boxing, mixed martial arts, kick boxing, self-defense, and personal fitness. 8.5 x 5.5, paperback, photos, illus, 208 pages.

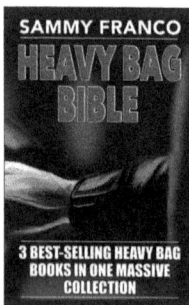

HEAVY BAG BIBLE
3 Best-Selling Heavy Bag Books In One Massive Collection
(Heavy Bag Training Series Books 1, 2, 3)
by Sammy Franco

In this unprecedented book collection, world-renowned martial arts and self-defense expert, Sammy Franco takes his thirty years of teaching experience and gives you the most authoritative information for mastering the heavy bag. The Heavy Bag Bible includes Franco's three best-selling heavy bag books collected into one huge paperback collection. This massive 530+ page book contains the entire Heavy Bag Training Series, books 1-3. 8.5 x 5.5, paperback, photos, illus, 538 pages.

DOUBLE END BAG WORKOUT
For Boxing, Mixed Martial Arts & Self-Defense
by Sammy Franco

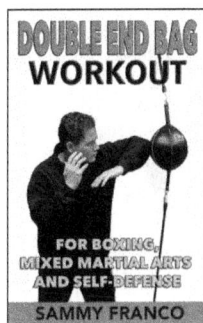

With over 200 detailed photographs, clear illustrations, and easy-to-follow instructions, Double End Bag Workout: For Boxing, Mixed Martial Arts and Self-Defense has everything you need to start training immediately. Double End Bag Workout also has beginner, intermediate and advanced workout routines that improve your speed, timing, accuracy, attack rhythm, and endurance. Whether you're an elite fighter or a complete beginner, this comprehensive book will take your boxing workout to the next level and beyond! 8.5 x 5.5, paperback, photos, illus, 260 pages.

THE COMPLETE BODY OPPONENT BAG BOOK
by Sammy Franco

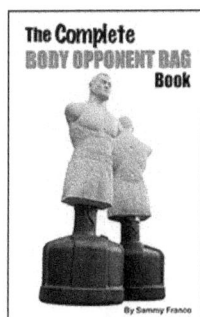

In this one-of-a-kind book, Sammy Franco teaches you the many hidden training features of the body opponent bag that will improve your fighting skills and boost your conditioning. With detailed photographs, step-by-step instructions, and dozens of unique workout routines, The Complete Body Opponent Bag Book is the authoritative resource for mastering this lifelike punching bag. It covers stances, punching, kicking, grappling techniques, mobility and footwork, targets, fighting ranges, training gear, time based workouts, punching and kicking combinations, weapons training, grappling drills, ground fighting, and dozens of workouts. 8.5 x 5.5, paperback, 139 photos, illustrations, 206 pages.

KNOCKOUT
The Ultimate Guide to Sucker Punching
by Sammy Franco

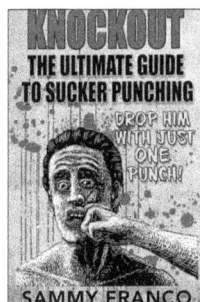

Knockout is a one-of-a-kind book designed to teach you the lost art and science of sucker punching for real-world self-defense situations. With over 150 detailed photographs, 244 pages and dozens of easy-to-follow instructions, Knockout has everything you need to master the devastating art of sucker punching. Whether you are a beginner or advanced, student or teacher, Knockout teaches you brutally effective skills, battle-tested techniques, and proven strategies to get you home alive and in one piece. 8.5 x 5.5, paperback, 244 pages.

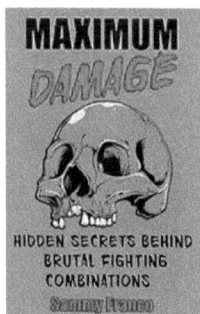

MAXIMUM DAMAGE
Hidden Secrets Behind Brutal Fighting Combinations
by Sammy Franco

Maximum Damage teaches you the quickest ways to beat your opponent in the street by exploiting his physical and psychological reactions in a fight. Learn how to stay two steps ahead of your adversary by knowing exactly how he will react to your strikes before they are delivered. In this unique book, reality based self-defense expert Sammy Franco reveals his unique Probable Reaction Dynamic (PRD) fighting method. Probable reaction dynamics are both a scientific and comprehensive offensive strategy based on the positional theory of combat. Regardless of your style of fighting, PRD training will help you overpower your opponent by seamlessly integrating your strikes into brutal fighting combinations that are fast, ferocious and final! 8.5 x 5.5, paperback, 240 photos, illustrations, 238 pages.

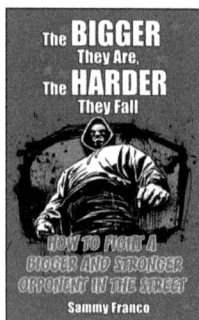

THE BIGGER THEY ARE, THE HARDER THEY FALL
How to Fight a Bigger and Stronger Opponent
by Sammy Franco

Sammy Franco was concerned that no book on the market successfully tackled the specific problem of fighting a larger, stronger opponent. In The Bigger They Are, The Harder They Fall, he addresses that all-important issue and delivers the solid information you'll need to win a street fight when the odds seem stacked against you. In this one-of-a-kind book, Sammy Franco prepares you both mentally and physically for the fight of your life. Unless you're a lineman for the NFL, there may come a day when you will face an opponent who can dominate you through sheer mass and power. Read and study this book before that day comes. 8.5 x 5.5, paperback, photos, illus, 212 pages.

CONTEMPORARY FIGHTING ARTS, LLC
"Real World Self-Defense Since 1989"
ContemporaryFightingArts.com